WAKE UP, AMERICA!
Noble "Kip" Caudill

All Rights Reserved ©2006 by Noble "Kip" Caudill
and The Caudill Charitable Foundation

No part of this book may be reproduced or transmitted in any form or by any means, graphic, electronic, or mechanical, including photocopying, recording, taping, or by any information storage retrieval system, without the permission in writing from the publisher.

Published by The Caudill Charitable Foundation

For information contact us at:
The Caudill Charitable Foundation
1000A Kendras Run
Gallatin, TN 37066

www.caudillfoundation.com

ISBN: 0-9779505-3-0

Printed in the United States of America.

Dedication

To the born again Christians of America and worldwide who follow the commands of Christ and who are fighting to restore Americas Godly heritage—I salute you.
—Kip

Wake Up, America!

Table of Contents

Wake Up, America!	9
Preface	15
Introduction	25

Section I: A City on a Hill

1	America's Religious Heritage	41
2	The True Meaning of the First Amendment	55
3	America Protected by God	67

Section II: Descent Into Darkness

4	The Threat	75
5	War Against Capitalism	81
6	War Against Christians	87
7	War Against Liberty	93

Section III: Who is Behind It?

8	Secular Humanism	99
9	Tools of the Secular Humanists: The ACLU	105
10	Tools of the Secular Humanists: Judges	111
11	Tools of the Secular Humanists: Educators	123
12	Tools of the Secular Humanists: Homosexual Activists	127

Section IV: What are the Effects?

13	Illegal Immigration	135
14	Families Destroyed	141
15	Children in Crisis	151
16	Undermining Our Military and War Effort	157
17	Balkanization of America	161

Section V: The War Outside

18	Radical Islam	171
19	Missile Defense	175
20	China	185
21	International Socialism and the United Nations	199

Section VI: Solutions

22	Returning to God	221
	What You Can Do	224
	Appendix	226

Wake Up, America!
★ ★ ★

America is by far the most blessed nation in the history of the world, with unprecedented opportunity in every endeavor of life available to her people at this present day. However, many believe she is in serious trouble, that she has lost her way, adrift in a sea of moral degradation.

A newspaper article claims that over 50% of the American population has suffered mental illness. Alcohol, illegal and prescription drugs are rampant. The divorce rate is at an all time high, the ghettos are virtual war zones. School systems are totally breaking down to the point that violence is an everyday way of life, where teachers literally fear for their lives, where scandal is everywhere. Our population has little or no respect for our political leadership. Our nation has nine trillion dollars in debt overhanging the U.S. economy and growing at the rate of one billion per day. The Social Security system is headed toward bankruptcy. Billions of hard-earned tax dollars have been spent on the welfare system since the 1960s, virtually creating no work ethic, fostering the birth of more children outside the family and your money wasted. Our media produces so much sleaze, filth, gossip, and violence that it is unthinkable to a decent citizen. Our nation's people are so stressed out that it is difficult to have a pleasant life. Many Americans are in such debt that they cannot pay for their lifestyle and are bitter about it. Murder, rape, and robbery are rampant; our judicial system is a massive failure. We incarcerate more criminals than almost any other country and are now the most violent nation on earth. The population is under attack by killer plagues like AIDS and the Avian Flu. Observing the majority of young people today, they look like slobs—our dress attire and demeanor is appalling, showing no self worth. Over 50% of the young people feel the future is hopeless and suicide is the number one teenage killer.

Wall Street is littered with stories of deceit and criminal activity fueled

WAKE UP, AMERICA!

by massive greed. Homosexuality is now an accepted alternative way of life in much of America. We now have a nation addicted to gambling, where casinos are opening up by the hundreds. Our people are being deceived by get-rich-quick state lotteries where we are being told the revenues will aid state governments (which of course justifies the means in their eyes). The Supreme Court has "discovered" the right to sodomy in our Constitution, and all of our elected officials continue to allow and condone the murder of unborn children by the millions each year.

In 1962, the liberal Supreme Court took the Bible and prayer out of America's school system, and what is the result we now have? Read any newspaper—total chaos!

Dear friend, you may not realize it, but the America you think you are a citizen of does not exist any more. If it is not dead already, it is dying fast. You had better wake up and realize the fact that the elected and appointed officials of this land have virtually sold We The People into slavery, socialism and yes, totalitarian communism. This so-called democratic government wants to nationalize healthcare and create a socialist monster that will wipe our yet another of your personal freedoms. And it won't stop there. Government will keep growing and invading every aspect of your life. Liberals literally want to control and monitor your every move. They want to destroy our armed forces and allow the United Nations to control our destiny. They will soon take away our tax-exempt status for churches that teach the Bible and your right to freely worship. God will be in such severe jeopardy that He could become an enemy of the state. They want to take away your right to bear arms and the Bill of Rights' guarantee to protect yourself.

This is not a picture of pre-World War II Nazi Germany under Hitler or the former Soviet Union; this is a picture of America today, and you are at risk whether you realize it or not.

These people who have done these deeds, those who have perpetrated their false secular-socialist doctrines upon our society, should be tried, convicted, and punished as traitors, tried for treason. They have murdered our Constitution and our Bill of Rights. You had better prepare for the battle if you still want to live in a free society, for the battle is coming and coming soon.

The people of this land who refuse to believe that we have a devastating problem, the liberal secular-socialists and those anti-God humanists who say that all is well and the future is bright, had better listen well.

The supreme God of the Holy Bible cannot and will not bless a Godless nation. The people who refuse to build their lives on God and the Lord Jesus Christ need to realize that are not only part of the problem, they are the problem. They are traitors to the liberty of a nation founded on the principles of God. We all need to realize the future for decency, honor, integrity, service to God and country, free enterprise, kindness, and peace of mind, peace and fellowship is not very bright indeed. There is only one solution now and forever: lives built on a solid rock foundation of Jesus Christ will build a rock solid nation. There is no other way. If our people do not have the courage to become "born again" perhaps they should leave this nation to those who are, and relocate in another country in Europe where they can practice their beliefs in the godless socialist atmosphere they so dearly love.

The church in America, those millions of souls who claim to be Christian, are far too often sitting placidly in stained glass buildings praising God, and spending the majority of our time and energy gossiping about the state of our nation and our Presidency. We criticize one another's denomination and form of worship and bask in the exclusivity of our great WORD and REVELATION knowledge, seemingly lacking the true love of Christ. All the while, Satan is literally devouring our land and cutting our forces to pieces. We had better wake up and get in this fight, this last and final fight of faith for the very heart and soul of the nation. There is no middle ground, no compromise, and no gray, passive land, dear friend. For this is an all-out war and you are either in the serv-

WAKE UP, AMERICA!

ice of the most high God or you are nothing, in compromise with the enemy. Thank God for those who will work to fulfill the commission that Christ gave to all who believe. Is it really that difficult to speak truthfully, be kind to people, give out Bibles, Christian tracts, audio and video tapes, financially support Godly people and causes, and be personally involved in the political and spiritual destiny of this nation?

This book will discuss America's founding as a religious nation, and how in the last 40 years the opponents of God and faith have fought a war to make the United States secular. It will also discuss other pillars of American greatness that are also under assault from many of the same forces lining up against Christianity. If Americans of faith don't wake up to the threat, the United States will be stripped of its greatest legacies—particularly the legacy of Christian morality in government.

To the reader, there are definite answers to what you can do to make a difference in America and have an impact in restoring America's Godly heritage.

1. Follow Christ with all your heart, mind, soul and strength.
2. Pray aggressively.
3. Read and meditate on the Bible daily.
4. Be a family person.
5. Gain knowledge on current events and our country's great history.
6. Be politically active and support Godly candidates.
7. Sponsor and promote Christian worldview events at your church or Bible study.
8. Actively write letters to the editors of your local media.
9. Contact your elected officials and let them know where you stand on crucial issues and how you want them to vote.
10. Give liberally to frontline organizations that fight the war on secular humanism.

The Caudill Charitable Foundation is a 501c3 tax deductible foundation that is committed to restoring America's godly heritage. We will fight for your interest and give an account of same.

Preface

★ ★ ★

JESUS CHRIST, THE SPIRITUAL AUTHOR OF THE DECLARATION OF INDEPENDENCE, THE U.S. CONSTITUTION, THE BILL OF RIGHTS, AND THE TRUE FOUNDER OF AMERICA.

The following treatise was written by John Chalfant, author of *"America: A Call to Greatness,"* perhaps the greatest book ever written for the cause of returning America back to her foundation principles of God in Christ—a book that should be read by every American citizen and taught in the schools and churches. I honor him as a great American patriot who has given his life for this effort and these principles. I strongly ask that you purchase this book and teach it to your family and friends. —*Kip Caudill*

THE PERSON OF CHRIST
I am the Alpha and the Omega, the Beginning and the End.—Revelation 1:8

In order for us to fully appreciate the priceless heritage handed down to us by America's Founding Fathers and the Source of the power of their faith, it is necessary to understand the central figure in the faith of the Founding Fathers from which they derived their wisdom, vision, and power. Let us, therefore, focus on Jesus Christ Himself and His complete uniqueness. He is available to us today through His Holy Spirit, just as He was to the Founding Fathers.

Could America Have Been Founded by Another Religion?
Today it is widely taught that "all religions are basically the same," that their prophets teach the same basic moral and legal codes. But, are they the same? Except for similar moral codes, can any "religion" be equated

Preface

to Christianity?

If so, why haven't other religions produced declarations of independence and constitutions that exalt and protect the individual, declared that he is created in the image of God and has a Divine right to be free, made the tyrant tremble, and rendered national military invincibility as did the Christian faith of the Founding Fathers?

What's the difference? Why and how does Christianity liberate men from the bondage of sin, corruption, and political tyranny while by historical and contemporary contrast other religions tend to subordinate the individual to harsh systems of freedom—denying legalism, or worse? The following commentary addresses these questions and was excerpted through items seven from *Many Infallible Proofs*, by Dr. Henry M. Morris.

The difference lies in the person of Christ. Biblical Christianity is absolutely unique in the nature of its central personage and founder, Jesus Christ. There is none other than Him in all of history or even in all literature. Some writers, of course, presume to place Christ as merely one in a list of great religious leaders, but this is absurd. He stands in contrast to all others, not in line with them, not even the head of the line. His uniqueness is illustrated in the following partial list of His attributes:

(1) Anticipation of His Coming. His coming was prophesied in fine detail as to lineage, birthplace, time, career, purpose, nature of death, resurrection, etc., hundreds of years prior to His actual appearance. There has never been any other religious leader—indeed, no other man—in all of history for which this was true.

(2) The Virgin Birth. Christ's virgin birth stands entirely alone; nothing like it was ever imagined elsewhere. God Himself took up residence in embryonic form in a virgin's womb, thence to be born in a fully natural human birth with no actual genetic connection to human parents.

(3) The Divine Human Nature. Although there have been power-crazed dictators and fanatics who have claimed to be God, even these individuals recognized and acknowledged that their assumption of divinity was only relative—they hardly imagined that they had created stars or even their own mothers! But Jesus Christ was God in the highest sense, the Creator of all things (see Col. 1:16), and He claimed to be God on many occasions and in many ways. He was also man in the fullest sense except that He had no sin. He was not half man and half God but rather all man and all God in a perfect and indissoluble union. No other man was ever thus—indeed, no other man ever claimed to be thus.

(4) Sinless. Of no one else in history could the claim ever be made in seriousness that he lived a while lifetime without one sin, in thought, word, or deed. But this very thing was claimed by Jesus' closest friends, by His worst enemies, by the greatest of the apostles, and by Jesus, Himself. Peter said, He did no sin (1 Peter 2:22), and John said, In him is no sin (1 John 3:5). Judas said, I have betrayed the innocent blood (Matt. 27:4), and Pilate said, I find in him no fault at all (John 18:38).

(5) Unique Teachings. The Sermon on the Mount is without parallel. The beauty and power of the Upper Room discourse, the compelling majesty of the Sermon on the Mount of Olives, the power of His parables, and all His other teachings are separated by a great gulf from even the finest teachings of other men. And yet His teachings continually include both the claim and the internal awareness that He was uniquely God's Son. In no other religious writings does one find such a phenomenon as this.

(6) His Unique Death. He said, It is finished, and he bowed his head, and gave up the ghost (John 19:30). Literally, He "dismissed His Spirit." It is evidently quite a difficult task even to commit suicide, but certainly

Preface

no one can simply decide to die and then, by his mere volition, proceed to die. But Jesus did! He said, No man taketh it from me, but I lay it down of myself (John 10:18).

(7) His Resurrection. Other religions of the world (including Islam, Buddhism, Hinduism, Confucianism, Animism, Shintoism, and Taoism, etc.) were founded by men who were, unlike Christ, sinful men. These founders are all in their graves, defeated by man's last enemy. Christ alone rose from the grave and defeated death.

What was it that so bound the Founding Fathers, the clergy, and the colonists together that they were empowered to function as a great, unified body in the common cause of liberty? It was the Spirit of the living, personal, eternal, omnipresent, omnipotent, loving, resurrected Christ. The Founding Fathers did not have to reach up to some impersonal God and try to please Him through their good works and through their obedience to a mass of brutalizing laws enforced by the tyranny of man.

Christ declared that He was and is God; I and my Father are one (John 10:30). He came personally to earth to dwell among us and teach us the way to personal salvation, to Spiritual and political freedom, and to life in all of its dimensions. He taught that God is our loving, caring Father, that He is accessible through prayer and will answer. Christ brought the relationship between man and God out of the abstract into one that is intimate, personal, and alive.

That's what we say about Him. But what did Christ say about Himself, directly and through His inspired apostles?

First let us distinguish Him from all other deities. Christ was part of the Trinity (One God in three Persons):

For there are three that bear record in Heaven, the Father, the Word (the Son), and the Holy Ghost (the Holy Spirit); and these three are one (1 John 5:7).

WAKE UP, AMERICA!

What is the Trinity? The concept that three equals one has long confused many Christians. There are several illustrations that help people cross that barrier: is such an abstract concept even possible? First use mathematics: instead of thinking 1+1+1, which clearly equals 3, ask how much is 1 _ 1 _ 1? Obviously, 1.

The Bible declares that things which cannot by seen can often be understood through nature. In fact, nature and our universe, including our very existence, are structured as trinities.

Consider, for example,
(1) Past, present, future: Take away any element. What is left?
(2) Space, mass, time: Take away any element. What is left?
(3) Length, width, breadth: Take away any element. What is left?

Examples from nature are innumerable. Consider Father, Son, and Holy Spirit. Suddenly the concept of a Triune Creator, one God in three persons, has entered the realm of feasibility because the principle of three-in-one is incontestably evident in nature. In fact with such evidence it could be argued that a triune God is more logical than a single God who created everything apart from His own nature, including man.

Who Is Jesus?
What did Jesus declare about Himself directly and through the prophets?

John 3:16 For God so loved the world, that he gave his only begotten Son, that whosoever believeth in him should not perish, but have everlasting life.

Rev. 1:8 I am the Alpha and Omega, the beginning and the ending, saith the Lord, which is, and which was, and which is to come, the Almighty.

John 1:1 In the beginning was the Word, and the Word was with God,

Preface

and the Word was God. He (the Word) existed in the beginning with, and as, God.

John 1:3 All things were made by him; and without him was not anything made that was made. The Creator.

John 1:4 In him was life; and the life was the light of men. The Source of life and light.

John 1:10 The world was made by him.

John 1:14 And the Word was made flesh, and dwelt among us…Christ was God incarnate (part of the Trinity).

John 1:14 …(and we beheld his glory, the glory as of the only begotten of the Father,) full of grace and truth.

John 14:6 I am the way… Christ is not assuming the role of a prophet and saying "God" is the way. He Himself claimed to be the way.

John 14:6 I am the truth… He declared Himself to be the truth.

John 14:6 I am the life… He declared Himself to be the life.

1 John 5:11 And this is the record, that God hath given to us eternal life, and this life is in his Son. He that hath the Son hath life. He declared Himself to be the Source of eternal life.

Ps. 119:142 Thy law is the truth… He declared Himself to be the Law.

John 17:17 Thy Word is truth… He declared Himself to be the Word.

Wake Up, America!

Ps. 119:151 Thy commandments are truth. He declared Himself to be the commandments.

John 15:1 I am the true vine, and my Father is the husband-man. He declared Himself to be the vine, the Father (God), the pruning caretaker.

John 15:15 I am the vine, ye are the branches… He declared His Divine relationship to man.

John 11:25 I am the resurrection, and the life…

John 11:25-25 He that believeth in me, though he were dead, yet he shall live… And whosoever liveth and believeth in me shall never die. He declared Himself to be the Source of eternal life.

Col. 2:2-3 …Christ; in whom are hid all the treasures of wisdom and knowledge. He declared Himself to contain all knowledge and wisdom.

Rom. 3:23-4 All have sinned, and come short of the glory of God; Being justified freely by his grace through the redemption that is in Christ Jesus. He declared that He has the power of redemption (to buy back for a price) and of justification (sinners absolved from sin).

Matt. 28:18 All power is given unto me in heaven and in earth. He declared that His power is total.

Matt. 9:6 The Son of man hath power on earth to forgive sins. He claimed, as only God can, to have the power to forgive sins.

John 8:12 I am the light of the world: he that followeth me shall not walk in darkness, but shall have the light of life. He declared Himself to be Light (Truth).

PREFACE

2 Cor. 3:17 Where the Spirit of the Lord is, there is Liberty. He declared Himself to be the Author of liberty.

Gal. 5:1 Stand fast therefore in the liberty wherewith Christ hath made us free, and be not entangled again with the yoke of bondage. Again, Christ declared Himself to be the Author of liberty. It is argued, correctly, that this verse refers to Spiritual liberty from the bondage of sin and corruption. But in the wake of Spiritual liberty comes the revelation and power of Truth, the mortal enemy of political tyranny. Irresistibly, when Truth gains its foothold, political freedom results.

John 8:32 Ye shall know the truth, and the truth shall make you free. Christ is truth.

Conclusion

Who was the real founder of America? Was it an assemblage of the Founding Fathers, the clergy, and the colonists? Was it an "expositor" of the Scriptures such as John Calvin, whose revolutionary insights crystallized into many of the freedoms we know today? Or was it Martin Luther, who broke the papal tyranny and began the Protestant Reformation? Perhaps it was the Reverend John Wycliffe who in 1382 helped bring the Dark Ages to a conclusion by translating the Bible from Latin into English for the common man and discovered in the Scriptures the principle of government, *"of the people, by the people, and for the people."*

In spite of their vast contributions that culminated in America's freedoms, none of these men ever claimed any role other than that of "expositor" or "translator" of the Bible. We can therefore draw no other conclusion than that Jesus Christ, beginning with the triumph of His resurrection, was the real Author of America's freedoms—the true Founder of America.

Clearly, Christ was the bedrock and centerpiece of the living, power-

WAKE UP, AMERICA!

filled (Spirit-filled) faith of the Founding Fathers, the colonists, and their clergy that brought forth our Declaration of Independence and our American Constitutional Republic.

Introduction

America is becoming a European country, and this is not a good thing. This is not to generalize that all Americans are becoming like all Europeans. But there are a whole host of disturbing forces—from within and without—that are pressing the United States as a nation more and more towards the models seen in France, Germany, and elsewhere, in what Secretary of Defense Donald Rumsfeld called "Old Europe".

There are three basic characteristics that have made Americans—and by extension, America—great over the centuries. These are an adherence to capitalism, a sense of liberty exemplified by rugged individualism, and a dedication to Godliness. But all three of these characteristics that have made us and our country great are under assault, and weakening day by day. As America's devotion to capitalism, individualism and Godliness have eroded, our nation has moved inexorably towards the modern socialist and atheistic models in Europe. Several years ago the constitutional scholar, Judge Robert Bork, wrote a book called, *Slouching Towards Gomorrah,* in which he points out that America was becoming an ever-increasingly immoral society. Judge Bork was exactly right. And he very ably discussed in detail how our country is moving away from the type of national character that made America great. We are slouching towards Gomorrah. We just weren't aware until this book that Gomorrah lays smack dab in the middle of France.

America has always been a capitalist nation, and this is a very good thing. The critics will claim otherwise, of course, but the simple fact is that no other economic system ever devised by mankind has created more wealth and prosperity for more people in the history of the world than capitalism. Fascism, communism, and all those other economic systems that have come down the pike have been nothing short of disastrous

INTRODUCTION

for the people that lived under them. But the capitalist system in America has made the vast majority of the people wealthier than any other people in history. Even our poorest Americans would be considered fabulously wealthy by historical standards. America should be proud to be a capitalist nation. But many elites in this country are embarrassed about capitalism. Instead, they are pressing for America to become more and more socialist, like the Europeans. And these elites are getting their wish. The single best indicator of socialist tendencies in a nation is the tax rate. There was a time not all that long ago when the United States didn't even have an income tax. Now our government is taking as much as half of your money every year to fund its great wealth re-distribution program. If this is not socialism, then what is? In this century, we could very easily see the United States with the same high taxes, high unemployment and stagnant economies as we see in Europe today. And if that happens, the greatest engine of economic development, innovation and wealth in the entire world—the U.S. economy—will be lost forever.

America has also been defined by our strong sense of rugged individualism. Our Founding Fathers created a nation and form of government that emphasized personal liberty above all. This emphasis on personal liberty has been a defining aspect of American culture. Because Americans value personal liberty and emphasize individualism so much, we have developed strong leadership and problem-solving capabilities. After all, it's easy to be ruled by others and told what to do with your life. It's hard to make your own decisions and deal with the consequences thereof all on your own. Because Americans have chosen this more difficult path of rugged individualism and personal responsibility, we have benefited greatly. You see it in what is called the "American work ethic." Few other peoples in the world have this sense of responsibility and dynamism. While many European nations once had a zeal for individualism, that notion has faded in the past century. Now, Europeans have handed their lives over to socialist caretakers in their own governments, and more recently to non-elected bureaucrats ruling over the European Union. They have taken the easier path, allowing others to rule in their stead. And America is following down that same path today. Where we once solved our own problems, Americans now increasingly allow a bigger and bigger federal government to take care of them. No clearer example of this can be seen than the aftermath of Hurricane Katrina in New Orleans. Tens of thousands of Americans simply sat by and waited for the government to take care of them. They waited for the government to tell them when to leave. They waited for the government to pick them up and take them out of town (and for many, the government was too late in evacuating New Orleans and failed to provide the transportation needed to remove the citizens when the decision to leave was finally made). And after the hurricane, those same American citizens waited for the government to feed them and clothe them and house them. This kind of thing never used to happen in the United States. When disaster struck—be it hurricane or tornado or earthquake or drought—Americans rallied together to take care of their own. Now fewer and fewer citizens even bother to help because they think like Europeans now. They say *"the government will take care of it."* But that's not how America, in its greatness, acts. We used to stand up and take the initiative to solve problems. Now we increasingly sit back and wait for someone else to do it. It's the same reaction you get from the Europeans. When Muslim terrorists attacked on 9/11, far too many Europeans sat on the sidelines and waited for America to fight these radicals. Some, like the socialist government in Spain, even adopted a strategy of appeasing the Muslim terrorists! Most of Europe can't be bothered to fight back against this dire Muslim threat to civilization. What happens if America gives up, too? What kind of world will we live in when murderous Islamic fanatics operate openly and freely in the world? It's the world we face if America slouches towards the European attitude.

Finally, and most importantly, America has been a great nation because

INTRODUCTION

Americans have traditionally been dedicated to God and His will. The Bible says that all the nations that forget God shall be turned into Hell. It used to be that an overwhelmingly large percentage of Americans were devoutly religious people who regularly attended church services every week. Because Americans were devoted to God, God in turn blessed our nation and its people. America went from a fledgling nation struggling to survive in a war with the greatest imperial power ever seen to the world's only superpower in just a matter of 225 years—a remarkably short span of history. How did this happen? Our Founding Fathers were firmly convinced that we were protected and guided by the divine hand of God. As William Penn, the founder of Pennsylvania said, *"Those who will not be governed by God will be ruled by tyrants."* In Europe, on the other hand, only a small minority of residents attend church. In fact, most of the many beautiful churches that dot the landscape of Europe are mere tourist attractions now, rather than functioning Houses of God. Sadly, this is happening more and more in America today. The forces of secularism and atheism have hammered away at traditional religion in America, and have weakened it substantially. God has been banned in public schools. The Ten Commandments are banned from our courtrooms. And those Americans who remain faithful to God are ridiculed every day by the anti-religious elites in this country. As a result, our national tradition of dedication to Godliness has waned. All you really need to do to see proof of this is to look at church attendance over the past forty-plus years—all the research shows that it's dropping rapidly. We our losing our faith as a country! And if this trend continues, America will abandon God just like the Europeans did. Were that to happen, we can be assured of two things: America will be ruled by tyrants, and our once-great nation shall be turned to Hell.

Contained within this book are an analysis of the institutions that make America great and the forces that are contributing to the downfall of these institutions. Also discussed are the international threats to our security that continue to grow while America's power continues to decline. And finally we present solutions for Christian Americans to save our great nation.

Section I: A City on a Hill

America is an exceptional nation, unlike any other on the planet. And our exceptionalism is exemplified by our faith, our economy, our adherence to liberty and individual freedom. America's exceptionalism allowed us to declare our independence from—and successfully fight a war against—the greatest empire the world had ever seen to that date. America's exceptionalism allowed us to survive a bloody civil war and remove once and for all the scourge of slavery that shamed our nation. America's exceptionalism gave us the power needed to rescue Europe in two World Wars, and save the world from fascism. And after that, America's exceptionalism gave us the strength to wage a forty-plus year Cold War to save the world from tyrannical Communism. No other nation on earth was capable, at each of these times in history, to overcome similar challenges. It was only the United States of America, that unique nation "under God," that rose to the challenge and succeeded time and time again against often seemingly insurmountable odds.

President Ronald Reagan often spoke of America's exceptionalism, referring to America as a City upon a Hill. We were the light in the darkness of the world. And no one articulated and championed America's exceptionalism as much or as well as Ronald Reagan. What follows are excerpts of the speech Ronald Reagan gave in 1974, when he first discussed the concepts of America as a City upon a Hill:

I thought that tonight, rather than talking on the subjects you are discussing, or trying to find something new to say, it might be appropriate to reflect a bit on our heritage.

You can call it mysticism if you want to, but I have always believed that there was some divine plan that placed this great continent between two

INTRODUCTION

oceans to be sought out by those who were possessed of an abiding love of freedom and a special kind of courage.

This was true of those who pioneered the great wilderness in the beginning of this country, as it is also true of those later immigrants who were willing to leave the land of their birth and come to a land where even the language was unknown to them. Call it chauvinistic, but our heritage does not set us apart. Some years ago a writer, who happened to be an avid student of history, told me a story about that day in the little hall in Philadelphia where honorable men, hard-pressed by a King who was flouting the very law they were willing to obey, debated whether they should take the fateful step of declaring their independence from that king. I was told by this man that the story could be found in the writings of Jefferson. I confess, I never researched or made an effort to verify it. Perhaps it is only legend. But story, or legend, he described the atmosphere, the strain, the debate, and that as men for the first time faced the consequences of such an irretrievable act, the walls resounded with the dread word of treason and its price—the gallows and the headman's axe. As the day wore on the issue hung in the balance, and then, according to the story, a man rose in the small gallery. He was not a young man and was obviously calling on all the energy he could muster. Citing the grievances that had brought them to this moment he said, *"Sign that parchment. They may turn every tree into a gallows, every home into a grave and yet the words of that parchment can never die. For the mechanic in his workshop, they will be words of hope, to the slave in the mines—freedom."* And he added, *"If my hands were freezing in death, I would sign that parchment with my last ounce of strength. Sign, sign if the next moment the noose is around your neck, sign even if the hall is ringing with the sound of headman's axe, for that parchment will be the textbook of freedom, the bible of the rights of man forever."* And then it is said he fell back exhausted. But 56 delegates, swept by his eloquence, signed the Declaration of Independence, a document destined to be as immortal as any work of man can be. And according to the story, when they turned to thank him for his timely oratory, he could not be found nor were there any who knew who he was or how he had come in or gone out through the locked and guarded doors.

Well, as I say, whether story or legend, the signing of the document that day in Independence Hall was miracle enough. Fifty-six men, a little band so unique—we have never seen their like since—pledged their lives, their fortunes and their sacred honor. Sixteen gave their lives, most gave their fortunes and all of them preserved their sacred honor. What manner of men were they? Certainly they were not an unwashed, revolutionary rebel, nor were then adventurers in a heroic mood. Twenty-four were lawyers and jurists, 11 were merchants and tradesmen, nine were farmers. They were men who would achieve security but valued freedom more.

And what price did they pay? John Hart was driven from the side of his desperately ill wife. After more than a year of living almost as an animal in the forest and in caves, he returned to find his wife had died and his children had vanished. He never saw them again, his property was destroyed and he died of a broken heart—but with no regret, only pride in the part he had played that day in Independence Hall. Carter Braxton of Virginia lost all his ships—they were sold to pay his debts. He died in rags. So it was with Ellery, Clymer, Hall, Walton, Gwinnett, Rutledge, Morris, Livingston, and Middleton. Nelson, learning that Cornwallis was using his home for a headquarters, personally begged Washington to fire on him and destroy his home—he died bankrupt. It has never been reported that any of these men ever expressed bitterness or renounced their action as not worth the price. Fifty-six rank-and-file, ordinary citizens had founded a nation that grew from sea to shining sea, five million farms, quiet villages, cities that never sleep—all done without an area redevelopment plan, urban renewal or a rural legal assistance program.

Now we are a nation of 211 million people with a pedigree that includes blood lines from every corner of the world. We have shed that

INTRODUCTION

American-melting-pot blood in every corner of the world, usually in defense of someone's freedom. Those who remained of that remarkable band we call our Founding Fathers tied up some of the loose ends about a dozen years after the Revolution. It had been the first revolution in all man's history that did not just exchange one set of rulers for another. This had been a philosophical revolution. The culmination of men's dreams for 6,000 years were formalized with the Constitution, probably the most unique document ever drawn in the long history of man's relation to man. I know there have been other constitutions, new ones are being drawn today by newly emerging nations. Most of them, even the one of the Soviet Union, contain many of the same guarantees as our own Constitution, and still there is a difference. The difference is so subtle that we often overlook it, but it is so great that it tells the whole story. Those other constitutions say, *"Government grants you these rights"* and ours says, *"You are born with these rights, they are yours by the grace of God, and no government on earth can take them from you."*

Lord Acton of England, who once said, *"Power corrupts, and absolute power corrupts absolutely,"* would say of that document, *"They had solved with astonishing ease and unduplicated success two problems which had heretofore baffled the capacity of the most enlightened nations. They had contrived a system of federal government which prodigiously increased national power and yet respected local liberties and authorities, and they had founded it on a principle of equality without surrendering the securities of property or freedom."* Never in any society has the preeminence of the individual been so firmly established and given such a priority.

In less than twenty years we would go to war because the God-given rights of the American sailors, as defined in the Constitution, were being violated by a foreign power. We served notice then on the world that all of us together would act collectively to safeguard the rights of even the least among us. But still, in an older, cynical world, they were not convinced. The great powers of Europe still had the idea that one day this great continent would be open again to colonizing and they would come over and divide us up.

In the meantime, men who yearned to breathe free were making their way to our shores. Among them was a young refugee from the Austro-Hungarian Empire. He had been a leader in an attempt to free Hungary from Austrian rule. The attempt had failed and he fled to escape execution. In America, this young Hungarian, Koscha by name, became an importer by trade and took out his first citizenship papers. One day, business took him to a Mediterranean port. There was a large Austrian warship under the command of an admiral in the harbor. He had a manservant with him. He had described to this manservant what the flag of his new country looked like. Word was passed to the Austrian warship that this revolutionary was there and in the night he was kidnapped and taken aboard that large ship. This man's servant, desperate, walking up and down the harbor, suddenly spied a flag that resembled the description he had heard. It was a small American war sloop. He went aboard and told Captain Ingraham, of that war sloop, his story. Captain Ingraham went to the American Consul. When the American Consul learned that Koscha had only taken out his first citizenship papers, the consul washed his hands of the incident. Captain Ingraham said, *"I am the senior officer in this port and I believe, under my oath of my office, that I owe this man the protection of our flag."*

He went aboard the Austrian warship and demanded to see their prisoner, our citizen. The Admiral was amused, but they brought the man on deck. He was in chains and had been badly beaten. Captain Ingraham said, *"I can hear him better without those chains,"* and the chains were removed. He walked over and said to Kocha, *"I will ask you one question; consider your answer carefully. Do you ask the protection of the American flag?"* Kocha nodded dumbly *"Yes,"* and the Captain said, *"You shall have it."* He went back and told the frightened consul what he had done. Later in the day three more Austrian ships sailed into harbor. It looked as

INTRODUCTION

though the four were getting ready to leave. Captain Ingraham sent a junior officer over to the Austrian flag ship to tell the Admiral that any attempt to leave that harbor with our citizen aboard would be resisted with appropriate force. He said that he would expect a satisfactory answer by four o'clock that afternoon. As the hour neared they looked at each other through the glasses. As it struck four he had them roll the cannons into the ports and had then light the tapers with which they would set off the cannons—one little sloop. Suddenly the lookout tower called out and said, *"They are lowering a boat,"* and they rowed Koscha over to the little American ship.

Captain Ingraham then went below and wrote his letter of resignation to the United States Navy. In it he said, *"I did what I thought my oath of office required, but if I have embarrassed my country in any way, I resign."* His resignation was refused in the United States Senate with these words: *"This battle that was never fought may turn out to be the most important battle in our Nation's history."* Incidentally, there is to this day, and I hope there always will be, a USS Ingraham in the United States Navy.

I did not tell that story out of any desire to be narrowly chauvinistic or to glorify aggressive militarism, but it is an example of government meeting its highest responsibility.

In recent years we have been treated to a rash of noble-sounding phrases. Some of them sound good, but they don't hold up under close analysis. Take for instance the slogan so frequently uttered by the young senator from Massachusetts, *"The greatest good for the greatest number."* Certainly under that slogan, no modern day Captain Ingraham would risk even the smallest craft and crew for a single citizen. Every dictator who ever lived has justified the enslavement of his people on the theory of what was good for the majority.

We are not a warlike people. Nor is our history filled with tales of aggressive adventures and imperialism, which might come as a shock to some of the placard painters in our modern demonstrations. The lesson of Vietnam, I think, should be that never again will young Americans be asked to fight and possibly die for a cause unless that cause is so meaningful that we, as a nation, pledge our full resources to achieve victory as quickly as possible.

I realize that such a pronouncement, of course, would possibly be laying one open to the charge of warmongering—but that would also be ridiculous. My generation has paid a higher price and has fought harder for freedom than any generation that had ever lived. We have known four wars in a single lifetime. All were horrible; all could have been avoided if at a particular moment in time we had made it plain that we subscribed to the words of John Stuart Mill when he said that, *"war is an ugly thing, but not the ugliest of things."*

The decayed and degraded state of moral and patriotic feeling which thinks nothing is worth a war is worse. The man who has nothing which he cares about more than his personal safety is a miserable creature and has no chance of being free unless made and kept so by the exertions of better men than himself.

The widespread disaffection with things military is only a part of the philosophical division in our land today. I must say to you who have recently, or presently are still receiving an education, I am awed by your powers of resistance. I have some knowledge of the attempts that have been made in many classrooms and lecture halls to persuade you that there is little to admire in America. For the second time in this century, capitalism and the free enterprise are under assault. Privately owned business is blamed for spoiling the environment, exploiting the worker and seducing, if not outright raping, the customer. Those who make the charge have the solution, of course—government regulation and control. We may never get around to explaining how citizens who are so gullible that they can be suckered into buying cereal or soap that they don't need and would not be good for them, can at the same time be astute enough to choose representatives in government to which they would entrust the

INTRODUCTION

running of their lives.

Not too long ago, a poll was taken on 2,500 college campuses in this country. Thousands and thousands of responses were obtained. Overwhelmingly, 65, 70, and 75 percent of the students found business responsible, as I have said before, for the things that were wrong in this country. That same number said that government was the solution and should take over the management and the control of private business. Eighty percent of the respondents said they wanted government to keep its paws out of their private lives.

We are told every day that the assembly-line worker is becoming a dull-witted robot and that mass production results in standardization. Well, there isn't a socialist country in the world that would not give its copy of Karl Marx for our standardization.

Standardization means production for the masses and the assembly line means more leisure for the worker—freedom from backbreaking and mind-dulling drudgery that man had known for centuries past. Karl Marx did not abolish child labor or free the women from working in the coal mines in England—the steam engine and modern machinery did that.

Unfortunately, the disciples of the new order have had a hand in determining too much policy in recent decades. Government has grown in size and power and cost through the *New Deal,* the *Fair Deal,* the *New Frontier* and the *Great Society*. It costs more for government today than a family pays for food, shelter and clothing combined. Not even the Office of Management and Budget knows how many boards, commissions, bureaus and agencies there are in the federal government, but the federal registry, listing their regulations, is just a few pages short of being as big as the Encyclopedia Britannica.

During the Great Society we saw the greatest growth of this government. There were eight cabinet departments and 12 independent agencies to administer the federal health program. There were 35 housing programs and 20 transportation projects. Public utilities had to cope with 27 different agencies on just routine business. There were 192 installations and nine departments with 1,000 projects having to do with the field of pollution.

One Congressman found the federal government was spending 4 billion dollars on research in its own laboratories but did not know where they were, how many people were working in them, or what they were doing. One of the research projects was, "The Demography of Happiness," and for 249,000 dollars we found that, *"people who make more money are happier than people who make less, young people are happier than old people, and people who are healthier are happier than people who are sick."* For 15 cents they could have bought an Almanac and read the old bromide, *"It's better to be rich, young and healthy, than poor, old and sick."*

The course that you have chosen is far more in tune with the hopes and aspirations of our people than are those who would sacrifice freedom for some fancied security.

Standing on the tiny deck of the Arabella in 1630 off the Massachusetts coast, John Winthrop said, *"We will be as a city upon a hill. The eyes of all people are upon us, so that if we deal falsely with our God in this work we have undertaken and so cause Him to withdraw His present help from us, we shall be made a story and a byword throughout the world."* Well, we have not dealt falsely with our God, even if He is temporarily suspended from the classroom.

When I was born my life expectancy was 10 years less than I have already lived—that's a cause of regret for some people in California, I know. Ninety percent of Americans at that time lived beneath what is considered the poverty line today; three-quarters lived in what is considered substandard housing. Today each of those figures is less than 10 percent. We have increased our life expectancy by wiping out, almost totally, diseases that still ravage mankind in other parts of the world. I doubt if the young people here tonight know the names of some of the diseases that were commonplace when we were growing up. We have more doctors per thousand people than any nation in the world. We have more

INTRODUCTION

hospitals that any nation in the world.

When I was your age, believe it or not, none of us knew that we even had a racial problem. When I graduated from college and became a radio sport announcer, broadcasting major league baseball, I didn't have a Hank Aaron or a Willie Mays to talk about. The Spaulding Guide said baseball was a game for Caucasian gentlemen. Some of us then began editorializing and campaigning against this. Gradually we campaigned against all those other areas where the constitutional rights of a large segment of our citizenry were being denied. We have not finished the job. We still have a long way to go, but we have made more progress in a few years than we have made in more than a century.

One-third of all the students in the world who are pursuing higher education are doing so in the United States. The percentage of our young Negro community that is going to college is greater than the percentage of whites in any other country in the world.

One-half of all the economic activity in the entire history of man has taken place in this republic. We have distributed our wealth more widely among our people than any society known to man. Americans work less hours for a higher standard of living than any other people. Ninety-five percent of all our families have an adequate daily intake of nutrients—and a part of the five percent that don't are trying to lose weight! Ninety-nine percent have gas or electric refrigeration, 92 percent have televisions, and an equal number have telephones. There are 120 million cars on our streets and highways—and all of them are on the street at once when you are trying to get home at night. But isn't this just proof of our materialism—the very thing that we are charged with? Well, we also have more churches, more libraries, we support voluntarily more symphony orchestras, and opera companies, non-profit theaters, and publish more books than all the other nations of the world put together.

Somehow America has bred a kindliness into our people unmatched anywhere, as has been pointed out in that best-selling record by a

WAKE UP, AMERICA!

Canadian journalist. We are not a sick society. A sick society could not produce the men that set foot on the moon, or who are now circling the earth above us in the Skylab. A sick society bereft of morality and courage did not produce the men who went through those years of torture and captivity in Vietnam. Where did we find such men? They are typical of this land as the Founding Fathers were typical. We found them in our streets, in the offices, the shops and the working places of our country and on the farms.

We cannot escape our destiny, nor should we try to do so. The leadership of the free world was thrust upon us two centuries ago in that little hall of Philadelphia. In the days following World War II, when the economic strength and power of America was all that stood between the world and the return to the dark ages, Pope Pius XII said, *"The American people have a great genius for splendid and unselfish actions. Into the hands of America God has placed the destinies of an afflicted mankind."*

We are indeed, and we are today, the last best hope of man on earth.

Section I: A City on a Hill

AMERICA'S RELIGIOUS HERITAGE

The United States of America is a Christian nation. The Declaration of Independence and Constitution are based on the Judeo-Christian ethic. The Holy Bible is the basis for our founding documents, and our system of laws. And America's leaders, from the Founding Fathers to politicians of today have made the point that America is a Christian nation. Now, this does not mean that all the people were or are Christian. But what it does mean is that Christian tenets were the basis for all of our founding documents, laws, moral codes and institutions.

There are many today who would argue that America is not a Christian nation. But an examination of just a few parts of American history clearly reveals that America is a Christian nation. Here are just a few examples:

- A portion of the Charter for the Virginia Colony said: *"To the glory of His divine Majesty, in propagating of the Christian religion to such people as yet live in ignorance of the true knowledge and worship of God."*

- When the Pilgrims signed the Mayflower Compact, they agreed: *"For the glory of God and advancement of ye Christian faith ... doe by these presents solemnly & mutually in ye presence of God and one of another, covenant & combine our selves together into a civil body politick."*

- Nearly all of the men who wrote the U.S. Constitution were professing Christians. (M.E. Bradford, A Worthy Company, Plymouth Rock Foundation., 1982).

- When Alexis de Tocqueville wrote his famous book on the great experiment in democracy by the United States, called Democracy in America, he said: *"In the United States of America the sovereign authority is reli-*

gious...there is no other country in the world in which the Christian religion retains a greater influence over the souls of men than in America."

- Abraham Lincoln, the man who kept our nation together, said: *"In regard to this Great Book, I have but to say, it is the best gift God has given to man. All the good the Savior gave to the world was communicated through this book. But for it, we would not know right from wrong. All things most desirable for man's welfare, here and hereafter, are to be found portrayed in it."* (George L. Hunt, Calvinism and the Political Order, Westminster Press, 1965, p.33)

And even the United States Supreme Court has stated that America is a Christian nation: *"Our laws and our institutions must necessarily be based upon and embody the teachings of the Redeemer of mankind. It is impossible that it should be otherwise; and in this sense and to this extent our civilization and our institutions are emphatically Christian...this is a religious people. This is historically true. From the discovery of this continent to the present hour, there is a single voice making this affirmation...we find everywhere a clear definition of the same truth...this is a Christian nation."* (Church of the Holy Trinity v. United States, 143 US 457, 36 L ed 226, Justice Brewer)

The *American Center for Law and Justice*, one of the most important religious freedom organizations in America, has made it equally clear that the United States is a religious nation:

"Our religious heritage is manifested in many ways that openly reflect government sponsorship and yet do not create an 'establishment' problem. The employment of congressional Chaplains to offer daily prayers in the Congress is a practice that has spanned two centuries. The government has recognized as national holidays days with undeniable religious significance, such as Christmas and Thanksgiving. 'In God we trust' is statutorily prescribed as our national motto to be inscribed on our currency. The language 'one nation under God' is included as part of the Pledge of Allegiance to the American flag. Congress has directed the President to proclaim a National Day of

WAKE UP, AMERICA!

Prayer each year. It is the current practice in every federal court to open proceedings with an announcement that concludes, 'God save the United States and this Honorable court.' A portrayal of the Ten Commandments decorates the courtroom of the United States Supreme Court, directly above the bench where the Honorable Justices are seated. As Justice Douglas observed, it is only through this accommodation that government can 'follow the best of our traditions' and 'respect the religious nature of our people.'" (Zorach v. Clauson, 343 U.S. 306, 314, 1952).

The Supreme Court has discussed the historical role of religion in our society and concluded that, *"[t]here is an unbroken history of official acknowledgment by all three branches of government of the role of religion in American life from at least 1789."* (Lynch v. Donnelly, 465 U.S. 668, 674, 1984). In Abington v. Schempp (374 U.S. 203, 212, 1963), the Court recognized that, *"religion has been closely identified with our history and government."* Such recognition is nowhere more affirmatively expressed than in Zorach where the Court stated that, *"[w]e are a religious people whose institutions presuppose a Supreme Being."* (343 U.S. at 313) Nevertheless, this country has witnessed a long struggle over governmental acknowledgments of the religious identity of the people of the United States.

The Founding Fathers and Nature's God

When in the course of human events it becomes necessary for one people to dissolve the political bands which have connected them with another and to assume among the powers of the earth the separate and equal station to which the laws of nature and of nature's God entitles them, a decent respect to the opinions of mankind requires that they should declare the causes which impel them to the separation.

Those are the words written by Thomas Jefferson in the Declaration of Independence. And the most important of these words to the Founding Fathers were those that declared the rights endowed to all mankind by "nature's God."

AMERICA'S RELIGIOUS HERITAGE

From the foundation of our country, America has relied on God and the rights bequeathed to us by Him. Thomas Jefferson made that crystal clear when he cited "nature's God" in the Declaration of Independence. And the other Founding Fathers made it equally clear in the Constitution of the United States when they guaranteed religious freedom in the First Amendment. But what is "nature's God," and what rights are granted by Him? The Founding Fathers clearly believed that nature was created by God, and that the Holy Scriptures contained the laws of God and the rights given to man by God.

From the time this country was founded, it was understood by our leaders that God had granted us certain rights that no government should curtail. It was also understood that, in order to continue to be a good and just nation in the eyes of the Lord, America must maintain that Christian heritage and give thanks to God for granting it to us. One of the first official acts of that Congress was to open in prayer. Virtually every President, upon taking the oath of office, invoked God in one way or another and asked Him to guide our nation. Congress also established a national day of Thanksgiving, praising God for granting our young nation its freedom.

But today, opponents of faith and prayer outrageously assert that the Founding Founders actually meant to strike God from the public domain when they approved the First Amendment to the Constitution. Such an assertion is blatantly false. The Founding Fathers explained that the First Amendment was merely to prevent a single denomination from being federally established. The Founders wanted to avoid in America what had occurred in Great Britain; all becoming—by government decree—Anglicans, Catholics, or any other denomination. Even the most superficial examination makes it clear that the Founding Fathers were devoutly religious men, and wanted their nation to be devoutly religious as well.

When America was founded, it was founded by Christians. In fact, 52 of the original 56 who signed the Declaration of Independence were avowed Christians. There were no Buddhists, Mormons, or Muslims present at that time. Those are simply the facts.

And these men were devoutly religious Christians, as well. It is as interesting as it is informative to look at some of the quotes from our Founding Fathers. These quotes indicate the founders' strong sense of Christian values and their perceived importance in the foundations of our nation:

George Washington: *"It is impossible to rightly govern without God and the Bible."*

John Adams: *"The general principles upon which our founders achieved independence… were the principles of Christianity."*

Andrew Jackson: *"The Bible is the rock upon which our republic rests."*

James Madison: *"Religion is the basis and foundation of government."*

James Madison: *"The future of America rests not in the laws of this Constitution, but in the laws of God."*

John Adams: *"Religion and virtue are the only foundations of free government."*

Patrick Henry: *"It cannot be emphasized too strongly or too often that this great nation was founded… by Christians; not on religions, but on the Gospel of Jesus Christ. The Bible is worth all other books that have ever been printed."*

Abraham Lincoln: *"The Bible is the best gift God ever gave to man."*
John Quincy Adams: *"From the day of the Declaration…[the American*

people] were bound by the laws of God, which they all acknowledge as the rules of their conduct."

James Madison: *"A nation that will not be ruled by the Ten Commandments shall be ruled by tyrants."*

James Monroe: *"The liberty, prosperity and happiness of our country will always be the object of my most fervent prayers to the Supreme Author of All Good."*

William Penn: *"Let men be good and government cannot be bad."*

There is even more historical evidence to substantiate America's religious heritage. The day after it approved the First Amendment and its protections of religious liberty, Congress called upon the president to *"recommend to the people of the United States a day of public thanksgiving and prayer, to be observed by acknowledging, with grateful hearts, the many favors of Almighty God."* President George Washington responded by proclaiming November 26, 1789 the first official day of Thanksgiving. In doing so, he said, *"It is the duty of all nations to acknowledge the providence of Almighty God, to obey his will, to be grateful for his benefits, and humbly implore his protection and favor."* John Adams, our second president, continued to support the tradition of giving thanks to God, saying, *"A day of solemn humiliation, fasting and prayer; that the citizens on that day abstain as far as may be from their secular occupations, [and] devote the time to the sacred duties of religion in public and in private."* Later, President James Madison, the Father of the Constitution and chief sponsor of the Bill of Rights, proclaimed that, *"The eyes of all should be turned to that Almighty Power, in whose hands are the welfare and the destiny of nations"* and recommended that citizens should address *"their vows and adorations to the great Parent and Sovereign of the Universe"* and *"render him thanks for the* many blessings he has bestowed on the people of the United States."

These statements of faith were not limited to our Founding Fathers, either. In 1944, President Franklin D. Roosevelt suggested, *"a nationwide reading of the Holy Scriptures during the period from Thanksgiving Day to Christmas"* so that the people *"may bear more earnest witness to our gratitude to Almighty God."* In fact, throughout our nation's history, our leaders have repeatedly invoked God and divine favor to protect our nation (Please see the appendix for invocations of God in every presidential inauguration speech).

The American Revolution—Why We Fought

Simply stated, we fought the American Revolution to get out from under an oppressive government (Great Britain) that controlled the fate of its citizens by not allowing any personal or economic freedoms for the average citizens. The government of Great Britain was a monarchy where the Royal Family was everything and the average person was nothing. The idea of "getting ahead" was not even a thought for the average person.

By contrast, our founders established America upon the principles of personal and economic freedom for its citizens. These freedoms were to be facilitated by a government that was to be for the people and by the people. In addition to a government that provided freedom for its people, the new nation of America provided economic opportunity through the free enterprise system and did not limit its citizen's opportunities, as do socialist societies or monarchies.

Free speech, freedom of press, the right to peaceably assemble, the right to seek a redress of grievances from the government and the freedom of religion were obviously top priorities in the minds of our founders. After all, these freedoms are part of what we see as a natural law, but were simply not part of the law for the citizens of Great Britain. These particular freedoms were of such great importance to our founders that they addressed them in the very First Amendment of our Bill of Rights.

AMERICA'S RELIGIOUS HERITAGE

Freedom of religion was first in the First Amendment because our Founding Fathers thought religious freedom should be paramount when they wrote the First Amendment.

The American Revolution was fought for the right to exercise our freedom and the right to life, liberty and the pursuit of happiness. One of the most important rights guaranteed to our people was the right to the free exercise of religion, or more accurately, to freely choose your denomination. When we consider the freedoms our forefathers fought for, against seemingly insurmountable odds, perhaps none are so fundamentally important nor as often discussed as the freedoms spelled out and provided by the First Amendment. Most will agree that America, the land of the free, was founded as a nation that was dedicated to the fact that all men are equal and have certain rights. In fact, the Declaration of Independence states that we are equal in the Laws of Nature and Nature's God…and that we are endowed by our Creator with certain unalienable rights, that among these are Life, Liberty and the Pursuit of Happiness. In other words, America was founded by a burning desire for freedom.

To assure a clear understanding of our freedoms, the founders developed the Bill of Rights and listed some of the most important, specific freedoms intended for all citizens. At the same time, the Bill of Rights also placed restraints upon the Federal Government by stating specific actions they are not allowed to take. At the time the Bill of Rights was enacted, states' rights were considered to be important, but nothing was more important than individual rights, as guaranteed by the constitution.

The Bill of Rights

The Bill of Rights is truly a remarkable document. It consists of the first Ten Amendments, represents the heart of our constitutional freedoms, is virtually all-inclusive, and precisely written. Yet all ten of these amendments can be printed upon less than two pages of an average size book.

The Bill of Rights was passed by the U.S. Congress on December 15,

WAKE UP, AMERICA!

1791. Some of the specific freedoms provided in the Bill of Rights include, free speech, free press, free exercise of religion; the right to keep and bear arms; freedom from unreasonable search and seizure; the right to not to testify against yourself; the right to not be deprived of life, liberty or property without due process of law; the right to not be subjected to double jeopardy; the right to just compensation for any property taken for public use; the right to a speedy and public trial by an impartial jury; the right to be informed of the nature and cause of the accusations; the right to have the assistance of counsel for your defense; the right to freedom from excessive bail and fines; the right to freedom from cruel and unusual punishment; and the freedom of each state to assume responsibilities for their own constitutions.

The Bill of Rights is fundamental to the understanding of the freedoms and liberties guaranteed to all American citizens. Note that the first ten amendments to the Constitution all guarantee individual rights, rather than enunciate any government rights vis-à-vis the people. Without the Bill of Rights, many of our God-given liberties—especially religious freedom—could have been jeopardized by the fledgling American government. These then are the First Ten Amendments to the Constitution; The Bill of Rights as ratified by the states:

Amendment I

Congress shall make no law respecting an establishment of religion, or prohibiting the free exercise thereof; or abridging the freedom of speech, or of the press; or the right of the people peaceably to assemble, and to petition the Government for a redress of grievances.

Amendment II

A well—regulated Militia, being necessary to the security of a free State, the right of the people to keep and bear Arms, shall not be infringed.

Amendment III

No Soldier shall, in time of peace be quartered in any house, without the consent of the Owner, nor in time of war, but in a manner to be prescribed by law.

Amendment IV

The right of the people to be secure in their persons, houses, papers, and effects, against unreasonable searches and seizures, shall not be violated, and no Warrants shall issue, but upon probable cause, supported by Oath or affirmation, and particularly describing the place to be searched, and the persons or things to be seized.

Amendment V

No person shall be held to answer for a capital, or otherwise infamous crime, unless on a presentment or indictment of a Grand Jury, except in cases arising in the land or naval forces, or in the Militia, when in actual service in time of War or public danger; nor shall be compelled in any criminal case to be a witness against himself, nor be deprived of life, liberty, or property, without due process of law; nor shall private property be taken for public use, without just compensation.

Amendment VI

In all criminal prosecutions, the accused shall enjoy the right to a speedy and public trial, by an impartial jury of the State and district wherein the crime shall have been committed, which district shall have been previously ascertained by law, and to be informed of the nature and cause of the accusation; to be confronted with the witnesses against him; to have compulsory process for obtaining witnesses in his favor, and to have the Assistance of Counsel for his defense.

Amendment VII

In suits at common law, where the value in controversy shall exceed twenty dollars, the right of trial by jury shall be preserved, and no fact tried by a jury, shall be otherwise reexamined in any Court of the United States, that according to the rules of the common law.

Amendment VIII

Excessive bail shall not be required, nor excessive fines imposed, nor cruel and unusual punishments inflicted.

Amendment IX

The enumeration in the Constitution, of certain rights, shall not be construed to deny or disparage others retained by the people.

Amendment X

The powers not delegated to the United States by the Constitution, nor prohibited by it to the States are reserved to the States respectively, or to the people.

As you can see, the Bill of Rights is the heart of our American freedoms that are so often taken for granted. The Constitution as a whole and the Bill of Rights specifically must be protected to insure that we know what the rules are, and for reference whenever our courts must make tough decisions, and yet do so with impartiality, common sense and fairness according to these rules and the law of the land. And the Founding Fathers knew that these rights were all derived directly from God. This is, fundamentally, what separates America from Europe. CNSNews.com summed this point up most concisely:

"According to recent findings by the Pew Global Attitudes Project, sponsored by the Pew Research Center for the People & the Press, 59 percent of Americans identified religion as an important part of their lives. In contrast,

11 percent of the French, 14 percent of Russians and 33 percent of Britons said religion was important to them."

"Europe is decidedly a post-Christian society," said Dr. Richard Lessner, executive director of the Family Research Council's American Renewal Project. "Faith is far less important in the daily lives of Europeans. Their institutions are not rooted in a particular faith point-of-view. They are thoroughly secular societies, with a very different national history from the national history of America."

True Meaning of the First Amendment

★ ★ ★

The Founding Fathers intended the citizens of the United States to have constitutionally guaranteed religious freedom, derived directly from God, and outlined in the Bill of Rights. In fact, the Founding Fathers believed that the source of our rights and freedoms come from the "laws of nature and of nature's God". That being the case, it seems clear to any rational person that public recognition of God, religion and morality would be protected by those same Founding Fathers. This point is even more acutely made by the fact that the First Amendment to the Constitution deals specifically with religious freedom.

But over the last forty-plus years, our religious freedom has been systematically curtailed—particularly by liberal judges. How did this happen? Well, it all started when the secular humanists began to corrupt the true meaning of the First Amendment to the United States Constitution.

The First Amendment is the most often quoted—and the most misunderstood—amendment in our Bill of Rights. The First Amendment is fundamental to the principles of freedom upon which our nation was founded and what we believe about America. But today, the original intent of the First Amendment has been seriously corrupted by years of liberal legal assaults. As a result, the bedrock foundation of our fundamental liberties has instead become a hammer to be used to smash religious freedom in America.

The Original Intent of the First Amendment

The purpose of the First Amendment, like all of the amendments that make up the Bill of Rights, were written amidst fears that certain privileges needed to be spelled out concerning the rights of the people. The First Amendment, like all of the amendments that make up the Bill of

TRUE MEANING OF THE FIRST AMENDMENT

Rights, was written amidst fears that government would intrude upon the rights of the people. The Founding Fathers wanted to know the government had restrictions that were clearly known, and that they the people were protected from the government. Thus, the First Amendment was written to place restrictions on the actions of the federal government.

However, the First Amendment was never meant to restrict free speech, freedom of press and the freedom to peaceably assemble. It also guarantees us the right to the free exercise of religion. The First Amendment begins with the phrase, *"Congress shall make no law respecting an establishment of religion, or prohibiting the free exercise thereof...."*. In other words, the First Amendment guarantees our right to freedom of religion, not from religion. America was not to become a country with a national religion, like England with its Anglican Church. The government was forbidden from establishing a national church. But the First Amendment was never intended to stamp out all vestiges of religion in public life. Unfortunately the prevailing liberal wisdom today is that the First Amendment means freedom from religion.

While the First Amendment provides citizens with some of our most important rights and freedoms, it also restricts Congress by placing specific limits upon their power. In other words, our Bill of Rights guarantees certain rights to our citizens and at the same time places certain limitations upon our government. In fact, if you look at the entire Bill of Rights from the previous chapter, it's clear that these amendments were intended to prevent government from limiting the liberties of our citizens, not the other way around. But if you look at how liberals interpret the First Amendment, they would have the government limit the religious expression of American citizens. This is in direct contradiction of the purpose of all amendments in the Bill of Rights.

The First Amendment is short, to the point and easy to understand. The First Amendment specifically guarantees citizens the right to the free exercise of religion and places specific limitations upon Congress in regard to the establishment of religion. The First Amendment begins, *"Congress shall enact no law respecting an establishment of religion."* Congress is restricted by the First Amendment which does not allow them to enact any law regarding the establishment of religion. That phrase, establishment of religion, is the so-called "establishment clause" which is so often quoted as precedence in court cases involving the issues that revolve around the freedom of religion.

The truth of the matter is, from the time the states ratified the First Amendment until just about 40 years ago, the rulings made by our courts were based upon a literal interpretation of the First Amendment. The First Amendment was applied exactly as it was written and exactly as our founders intended. However, the original and clearly intended meaning of the First Amendment has been corrupted and changed into an argument that is a perverse mockery of what our founders intended.

The Assault on Original Intent

Under direct and relentless legal pressure from groups such as the American Civil Liberties Union (the notorious ACLU, a radical leftist group that files lawsuits to promote its anti-Christian agenda), Americans United for Separation of Church and State, and other anti-religious groups, liberal courts have decided that government, at every level, must remain "neutral" toward religion. But rather than not promoting one religion over another, the liberal judges have ruled that government must not advance any religion ever—even though it's clear that the Establishment Clause of the First Amendment was never intended to prohibit government from advancing religion. On the contrary, it is clear that the Founding Fathers believed only a moral and religious nation could remain free. They thought it essential that government take an active role in promoting the moral character of the American people. In just one of numerous examples, the first Congress passed the Northwest Ordinance, which stated, *"Religion, morality, and knowledge, being neces-*

TRUE MEANING OF THE FIRST AMENDMENT

sary to good government and the happiness of mankind, schools and the means of education shall forever be encouraged." This clearly follows the intent of the Constitution—to promote religion and morality in general without promoting any one particular religious denomination. In another example, George Washington, in his first speech as president, appealed to the *"Almighty Being who rules the universe"* for the success of the government of the United States. If the ACLU was around back in President Washington's day, they probably would have filed a lawsuit against him for uttering those words!

One of the most important battles the ACLU fought in recent memory was that against Alabama Chief Justice Roy Moore. Chief Justice Roy Moore had a Ten Commandments display installed in the Alabama Supreme Court building after his election, as a way for the people of his state to acknowledge God and His role in establishing our laws. The ACLU went ballistic against Chief Justice Moore and his Ten Commandments display, and filed a lawsuit against it. This became one of the preeminent Religious Freedom legal battles in recent memory. And few people in America were better equipped than Chief Justice Moore to defend the true meaning of the First Amendment.

Judge Moore wrote a strong defense of his position in an article called Religion in the Public Square, published in 1999 by the Cumberland Law Review. Excerpts of this article are an excellent summary of the Religious Freedom battle in America today. Chief Justice Roy Moore deals effectively with the First Amendment, the Establishment Clause, Separation of Church and State, defining Religion as a matter of free will choice, the public display of the Ten Commandments and voluntary school prayer: *"The real purpose of the First Amendment was and is to protect the states' and their citizenry's right's to acknowledge God according to the dictates of their conscience. If not for a desire to protect this unalienable right, the First Amendment would not have been ratified."*

WAKE UP, AMERICA!

Since the *Alabama Freethought Association's* constitutional challenge to my actions in 1995, the debate has raged over whether such practices are permitted under the First Amendment. Throughout the debate my position on the matter has not only remained unchanged, but has even been bolstered by the ongoing discovery of the historical evidence and legal scholarship supporting my position.

The display of the Ten Commandments in the Etowah County courtroom and the court's practice of opening jury organizational session in voluntary prayer have as their purpose the acknowledgement of that God upon whom the laws and government of the United States are based. Some may recoil at the forthright proposition that recognition by the state of the sovereignty of God does not violate the Constitution; however, an examination of the evidence clearly demonstrates that objections to official state acknowledgements of God are only a recent phenomenon in United States history. The purpose of this article is to examine the history, purpose, and meaning of the term "religion" as used in the First Amendment's Establishment Clause and Free Exercise Clause, and the common misconceptions and misunderstandings surrounding that term. This article will also explain why the acknowledgement of God is the very object and purpose of the First Amendment.

What did our forefathers intend by prohibiting Congress from passing laws, *"respecting an establishment of religion"* but also prohibiting Congress from passing law, *"prohibiting the free exercise thereof"*? To answer this question, it is essential that we know how the drafters of the First Amendment defined the word "religion."

Madison clearly defined religion as, *"the duty which we owe to our Creator, and the manner of discharging it, [which] can be directed only by reason and conviction, not by force or violence."*

In sum, religion encompasses all of the duties owed to God and the manner of discharging those duties, both of which depend solely on individual conscience. Such duties to God were secured as rights against

TRUE MEANING OF THE FIRST AMENDMENT

any laws prohibiting their performance.

According to Madison, all men are subject to God, and their duty to Him is superior to that owed to civil government simply because government authority is ordained by God. This, civil government was not to become entangled in questions of religion, or the duties which we owe to our Creator and the manner of discharging those duties. For this reason our forefathers declared that Congress shall make no law respecting the establishment of the duties which we owe to our Creator and the manner of discharging those duties. As the framers understood the term religion, there is no clash between the Establishment Clause and the Free Exercise Clause.

Succinctly stated, the First Amendment Establishment Clause was never intended to eliminate the necessary truth that government must recognize the sovereignty of God. To the contrary, God's sovereignty over nations is the very basis of the First Amendment religion guarantees, and without such sovereignty, these guarantees could not exist.

Although the phrase "wall of separation between church and state" does not appear in the Constitution of the United States, Declaration of Independence, Articles of Confederation, or any other official American document, many American have been led to believe that the First Amendment Establishment Clause requires our government to separate itself from anything relating to God. Such an interpretation of the meaning of religion clauses of the First Amendment is simply erroneous.

Herein lies the true meaning of separation of church and state-government may never dictate one's form of worship or articles of faith. This does not mean that all public worship of God must be stopped; on the contrary, the free public worship of God was the very reason for a doctrine of separation of church and state.

Chief Justice Rehnquist said that *"the 'wall of separation between church and state' is a metaphor based on bad history, a metaphor which has proved useless as a guide to judging. It should be frankly and explicitly abandoned."*

WAKE UP, AMERICA!

Rehnquist also noted that *"the greatest injury of the 'wall' notion is its mischievous diversion of judges from the actual intention of the drafters of the Bill Of Rights."*

Arguably, the doctrine has been abused, twisted, and taken out of context in recent Supreme Court decisions in order to prohibit the public worship of God.

In 1878, the Supreme Court agreed with [Thomas] Jefferson's belief that the proper role of government did not encompass dictating how people should think or what they could or could not believe.

On the other hand, denial of the right to worship God in public institutions and by public officials would have been an unconstitutional intrusion because it would have been a denial of the freedom of conscience.

Some have argued that public prayer coerces unwilling citizens to participate. In the recent DeKalb County school prayer case, the United States District Court for the Middle District of Alabama held that student prayer at a graduation ceremony, *"may be effectively coercing students who do not wish to hear or participate in prayer to do so…"*

To the contrary. The only coercion that has taken place in the DeKalb County school prayer case is a federal court order forbidding such activities. The Christian majority has been coerced into silence, simply because the minority might have to hear them. But nothing in the U.S. Constitution guarantees that a student will never have to hear disagreeable or offensive views because that student might feel peer pressure to participate. Peer pressure or public opinion are not the types of coercion the Framers intended to prohibit. By its plain text, the First Amendment only forbids the enactment of "any law."

No student should ever be forced by law to participate in prayer, but to stop the acknowledgement of God by prayer simply because another student might listen to something he does not wish to hear is as illogical as eliminating a school's mascot or motto because it may offend a student. Likewise, to conclude that student-led prayer before a football game is a

TRUE MEANING OF THE FIRST AMENDMENT

pervasive religious activity and coercive is really but the intrusion of the federal magistrate's power into the field of opinion.

When the First Congress met in April 1789, one of their first actions was to appoint chaplains in both Houses of Congress. From April 1789 to this date, Congress has recognized God by the appointment and payment from government funds of a chaplain to open each House of Congress and each session with prayer.

John Jay, in May 1790 specifically authorized opening courts sessions with prayer by invited clergy. There after, all of the early justices of that Court observed that practice. Even today the United States Supreme Court opens with prayer.

Our forefathers clearly intended to base our government on a belief in God and believed that schools were the proper place to encourage religions and moral development.

Since the early 1960's when prayer and Bible reading in public schools were excluded by the Court, there has been a consistent effort to remove any recognition of God from public schools and public life. In 1962, when the United States Supreme Court removed the twenty-two word prayer of the New York Board of Regents in Engle v. Vitale, the Court completely ignored precedent, failing to cite one case in support of its decision.

How did the Supreme Court accomplish this feat, transforming the original intent of America's founders into a rule of its own making according to its own intent? Simply stated, the court did so by changing the role of the judiciary in American government, departing from the original intent of a judicial branch limited to saying what the law is, to making the law case-by-case.

The Court exceeded the authority of the judiciary by declaring the law to conform to their personal view of what the world should be. They chose to declare what the law should be, as opposed to what the law is, based upon fixed absolute standards.

WAKE UP, AMERICA!

For over one hundred seventy years before 1962, prayer had occurred in the schools of our land; yet without the citation of a single case, that practice was abruptly ended.

Yet neither the federal law nor the First Amendment has changed. All that has changed is the Supreme Court's attitude towards official acknowledgments of God. Beginning with the 1960 prayer and Bible reading cases and continuing with various additional ruling demanding religious neutrality in the public square, the Court has substituted its intent for that of the Framers and of Congress and the President. If this judicial trend continues, soon the intentions of a few will become the deception of many.

From the beginning, prayer in school was a regular practice across our land. Only by ignoring history in the Engel case was the Court able to cast the regular practice of school prayer lightly aside.

To this day, prayers similar to that composed by the New York Board of Regents continue to be made in the halls of state legislatures and Congress, at inaugurations of Presidents and Governors and in America's courtrooms, including the United States Supreme Court. Indeed, the impeachment trial of President Clinton began in the United States Senate with an invocation by the Senate Chaplain seeking God's guidance.

By depriving America's school children of the privilege of prayer, the Court has not stopped a first experiment on their liberties, but denied to public school children the right to engage in a civic activity that goes to the very heart of the American way of life, reflected in the nation's motto, *"In God We Trust."*

In 1962, and to this day, the United States Supreme Court has usurped the power of the states to acknowledge the Creator, a power and right preserved to the people under the First and Tenth Amendments of the United States Constitution. In doing so, the Court has directly contradicted the wishes of the people expressed by Congress in 1954, 1955, and 1956. In case after case, the Supreme Court has incorrectly held that

TRUE MEANING OF THE FIRST AMENDMENT

a connection between state government and God is inappropriate. It is time now to pay heed to the words of Madison, which Justice Black ignored in *Engel*: *"The freemen of America did not wait until usurped power had strengthened itself by exercise and entangled the question in precedents. They saw all consequences in the principle and they avoided the consequences by denying the principle. We revere this lesson too much, soon to forget it."*

When government interferes in any way with man's dutiful relationship with God, it interferes with freedom of conscience. The First Amendment to the United States Constitution was adopted to preserve the right to worship God according to the dictates of conscience and to prevent government interference with that right.

The intent of our Founders was never to prohibit the public acknowledgment of God, for to do so would have been a denial of the basis upon which our freedoms are secure. To restrict a display of the Ten Commandments in a court of law, to forbid opening courts with prayer, or to deny children the right of voluntary participation in prayer is a denial of the acknowledgment of God in violation of the United States Constitution and the First Amendment.

Chief Justice Moore's words make it very clear that our Constitution was based upon the idea of freedom for all Americans. The First Amendment says that we have Freedom of Speech, Freedom of Press and Freedom of Religion. How can we say we have Freedom of Religion in America when the courts do not allow the public acknowledgement God?

There is a huge difference between the establishment of religion and the acknowledgement of God. Posting the Ten Commandments no more establishes a religion than a statue of Buddha establishes Buddhism. Therefore, neither the placing of the Commandments in public, nor placing a statue of Buddha can be said to represent an establishment of religion. These events do not represent the establishment of religion, but rather the acknowledgement of religion. And that is the fundamental and real meaning of the First Amendment.

In conclusion, the Establishment Clause was meant to prevent the establishment of an official religion in America. This Establishment Clause would protect minority religious rights in America by ensuring that no establishment religion ruled the day. But thanks to the ACLU and their liberal judge allies, the exact opposite is true today. Today, thanks to the perversion of the First Amendment, a small minority of tyrannical atheists have imposed their will on the vast majority of Americans who believe in God.

AMERICA PROTECTED BY GOD

For most of America's history, the citizens of this country believed that the United States has had special protection from God. This belief stemmed directly from the fact that America was an exceptional nation, reverent to God and striving in all things to serve God's will. Not only do many Americans believe that God protects the United States, most Americans believe that our nation's deep religious faith is the basis for our country's great economic, military and cultural success over the centuries. Pew Research Center reports that, even today, nearly six in ten Americans (58%) think the strength of American society is based on the religious faith of its people. And two-thirds of the American people consider the United States to be a Christian nation. But disturbingly, the other third of the country takes the opposing view, that the society would be strong even if most Americans did not have a religious faith. And the trend in America is moving more and more away from God and faith—towards the atheistic point of view.

In the last 50 years, after suffering assault after assault against religion and morality in America, it is clear that people in this country, especially young people, lack the morals Americans once had. Pew Research Center reports that in 1952, half of Americans saw no decline in public morals, and 57% said young people had as strong a sense of right and wrong as did the youth fifty years previously. Today, just 21% think Americans on the whole are as honest and moral as in the past, and an equally small number (19%) think that young people have the same sense of right and wrong as 50 years ago. These Americans are correct in their assessment. And unless this terribly dangerous trend is reversed soon, America will degenerate into an irreligious European-type nation, where religion is considered a relic of the past. But this would be a disaster for the country and all of us living in it.

AMERICA PROTECTED BY GOD

When America was created by our Founding Fathers, it was dedicated to God. America was governed by the Bible and our belief in righteousness. An examination of virtually any of the founding documents (Declaration of Independence, Constitution, Bill of Rights, Federalist Papers, etc.) makes this clear. The Bible clearly states that righteousness exalts a nation and sin is a reproach to any people. Because America was a righteous nation, God put a wall of protection around the United States.

For centuries, America honored God, our children prayed in school, our families stayed together, and we went to church. In return for our good faith, God protected and rewarded us. There has never been a country as rich, as powerful, or open to opportunity for all people than America. America has been blessed with bountiful riches and divine protection. America's God-fearing way of life was a blessing to our land for most of our history.

But tragically, that is all changing today. Immorality is spreading across the country. Pornography is the number one industry on the internet. Our families are being ripped apart because of rampant divorce. A tragically large number of Americans are addicted to drugs and alcohol - and far too many of them are children abandoned by one or more parent. Thanks to liberal judges imposing their will on the rest of us, prayer has been banned in school. The Ten Commandments have been torn from every aspect of public life. The wisdom of the Bible has been taken away from our children. The ACLU has filed lawsuits against the Boy Scouts—a religious organization that pledges allegiance to God and strives to be "morally straight"—to force them to accept homosexual Scoutmasters. And thanks to a recent Supreme Court decision, even homosexual sodomy has become a protected right in America. This is all a painful insult to God. As Evangelist Pat Robertson lamented on the decline of morals in America, *"We don't want to be associated with the righteous beginnings of this nation any longer. We want to build our nation upon decadence, deception and violence."*

WAKE UP, AMERICA!

The worst of all of these great moral tragedies is the holocaust of abortion. Over 40 million babies have been killed in the abortion mills of America since Roe v. Wade was adopted as law. In America, we've killed more human beings than Hitler, Stalin or Mao Tse Tung every dreamed possible. And we're allowing it to happen all in the name of "personal choice" and "privacy rights." Well, even if any of us made the "personal choice" to kill another person, we couldn't escape from either God's law or the law of the United States by claiming it was a matter of "privacy." So why in the world does America allow the horror of murderous abortion to continue? And how in the world can we expect to experience God's divine blessings and protection as a nation anymore?

God's wall of protection that has surrounded the United States from its founding is beginning to crumble. God has been more than patient with us, but America continues to thumb our noses at the Lord. And the future repercussions will not be pleasant. For example, the 9/11 terrorist attacks, as bad as they were, could have been much worse. Terrorists already have, or will soon, get their hands on biological, chemical or even nuclear weapons. Imagine how many Americans will die if a weapon of mass destruction is detonated in the heart of an American city? Millions could die in an instant, and millions more would be horribly wounded. Our government is doing its best to prevent such a horrific attack on American soil. But our government is not perfect. And it only takes one mistake to allow the terrorists to sneak a weapon of mass destruction into the country and set it off in a major American city. Our only chance as a nation is to put our faith and trust in the only infallible form of protection—that which comes from God. God can protect America from a devastating terrorist attack carried out with weapons of mass destruction. But because America is rejecting God more and more, we can no longer be sure He will protect us.

Section II: Descent into Darkness

America is on the decline. Of that there is no doubt. We as a nation are descending into darkness, and the evidence for this abounds.

William J. Bennett, one of the leading conservative social commentators in America, has studied in detail the decline of America in stark terms for us. He concludes the following in a Wall Street Journal article: "*Perhaps no one will be surprised to learn that, according to the index, America's cultural condition is far from healthy. What is shocking is just how precipitously American life has declined in the past 30 years, despite the enormous government effort to improve it.*"

Since 1960, the U.S. population has increased 41%; the gross domestic product has nearly tripled; and total social spending by all levels of government (measured in constant 1990 dollars) has risen from $143.73 billion to $787 billion—more than a fivefold increase. Inflation-adjusted spending on welfare has increased by 630%, spending on education by 225%.

But during the same 30-year period there has been a 560% increase in violent crime, a 419% increase in illegitimate births; a quadrupling in divorce rates; a tripling of the percentage of children living in single-parent homes; more than a 200% increase in the teenage suicide rate; and a drop of almost 80 points in SAT scores.

Clearly many modern-day social pathologies have gotten worse. More important, they seem impervious to government's attempts to cure them. Although the Great Society and its many social programs have had some good effects, there is a vast body of evidence suggesting that these "remedies" have reached the limits of their success.

Perhaps more than anything else, America's cultural decline is evidence of a shift in the public's attitudes and beliefs. Social scientist James Q. Wilson writes that, "*the powers exercised by the institutions of social control have been constrained and people, especially young people, have embraced an ethos that values self-expression over self-control.*" The findings of pollster

WAKE UP, AMERICA!

David Yankelovich seem to confirm this diagnosis. Our society now places less value than before on what we owe to others as a matter of moral obligation; less value on sacrifice as a moral good; less values on social conformity and respectability; and less value on correctness and restraint in matters of physical pleasure and sexuality.

William Bennett is not alone in his alarm. According to Bennett, when the late Walker Percy was asked what concerned him most about America's future he answered: *"Probably the fear of seeing America with all its great strength and beauty and freedom…gradually subside into decay through default and be defeated, not by the Communist movement demonstrably a bankrupt system but from within by weariness, boredom, cynicism greed, and, in the end, helplessness before its great problems."*

Alexander Solzhenitsyn in a speech earlier this year put it this way, *"The West…has been undergoing an erosion and obscuring of high moral and ethical ideals. The spiritual axis of life has grown dim."* John Updike has written, *"The fact that compared to the inhabitants of Africa and Russia, we still live well cannot ease the pain of feeling we no longer live nobly."*

Author La Shawn Barber has also written about the decline of America. He says, *"In The Decline and Fall of the Roman Empire, author Edward Gibbon discusses several reasons for the great civilization's demise, including the undermining of the dignity and sanctity of the home and the decay of religion."*

America has been compared to the Roman Empire in secular and religious ways. Regardless of its ultimate legacy, America is a civilization on the decline. A couple of centuries from now (or sooner), someone will write a book called, *"The Decline and Fall of the American Empire."* Historians will lament the loss of a once-great civilization that brought prosperity to the world and tried to make it safer for democracy. The glory that was the United States will lay in ruins, brought down not by terrorists but its own debauchery and complacency.

AMERICA PROTECTED BY GOD

Back in 1947, a social scientist named Carle Zimmerman reviewed the decline of a number of civilizations and empires, and found several common trends that signaled imminent decline in a society:

- Decline of marriage as an institution.
- A rise in feminism.
- Public disrespect for parents and authority in general.
- Increases in juvenile delinquency and promiscuity.
- Decline in acceptance of family responsibilities.
- Acceptance of adultery.
- Increases in sexual perversions and sex-related crimes.

Is it not painfully clear that these common trends afflict America today? The answer is, of course, yes. And that means the decline of America is well underway. Look at the terrible decline of the sacred institution of marriage, as just one example. Marriage and the traditional family are under direct assault from big government (replacing fathers with welfare payments), homosexual activists (promoting gay marriage) and the tax system (imposing a marriage penalty tax). As a result of this war against the institution of marriage, our country is suffering the terrible results.

One expert, David Popenoe, in his testimony before the Committee on Ways and Means in the United States House of Representatives, put the damage in these stark terms:

As the recent results of the Year 2000 Census confirm, marriage as the basis of family life continues to decline in America. Since 1970 the rate of marriage has dropped by about one third, the out-of-wedlock birth ratio has climbed from 11% to 33% of all births, the divorce rate has doubled, and the number of people living together outside of marriage has grown by over 1000%. With the exception of non-maritial cohabitation, which increased dramatically, the marriage-decline trends decelerated a little in the 1990s. But they have continued in the same direction.

WAKE UP, AMERICA!

As of now, there is no tangible evidence of a turnaround, although a more pro-marriage attitude does seem to be gaining ground in the media and the culture at large.

Why should this marriage decline be of national concern? Principally, because of its effects on our nation's children. The social science evidence is now overwhelming that children fare better in life if they grow up in a married, two-parent family. Children who grow up in other family forms are two to three times at greater risk of having serious behavioral and emotional problems when they become adolescents and adults. Many of today's youth problems can be attributed, directly or indirectly, to the decline of marriage. This includes high rates of juvenile delinquency, suicide, substance abuse, child poverty, mental illness, and emotional instability. One important new study has found that the average American child in recent decades reported more anxiety than child psychiatric patients in the 1950s. Indeed, as former Senator Moynihan once observed, the United States, *"may be the first society in history in which children are distinctly worse off than adults."*

Sadly, the examples of American societal decline don't end with just marriage. In nearly every quantifiable category, the United States is in deepening trouble. How did this happen? How did the greatest, most powerful and morally just nation on earth fall so hard so fast? The answer is simple: America's traditional institutions have been under constant assault from within, eroding that which makes the United States great. And unless Americans wake up to the danger now, the damage will so be irreversible.

Section II: Descent into Darkness

THE THREAT

There is a war going on in the United States. On one side of this war are the forces of secularism and socialism, led by the American Civil Liberties Union. On the other side of this war are traditional Christian Americans who believe in capitalism, liberty and religious faith. Over the last forty-plus years, the secular-socialists have waged an unceasing battle against traditional American values, with few if any counter-attacks from the traditional American side. As a result, there has been a dangerous eroding of the three fundamental pillars of American society—capitalism, liberty and religious faith. And if traditional Americans do not wake up to this dire threat from the secular-socialists, the United States will be stripped entirely of that which makes us as a great nation.

America is a capitalist nation. Capitalism may have a bad name with liberal elites here at home and European socialists overseas, but the fact is that there has never been a greater economic system invented in human history. Capitalism, as opposed to socialism, promotes and rewards merit and talent with financial gain. The profit motive rewards those who strive to be successful in business. And when people are successful in business, many others benefit. Jobs are created. Goods and services are provided to make life easier. And there is even more money available for the government to fund those legitimate roles it should perform. On the other hand, socialism destroys innovation, punishes success, and deflates an economy.

Look at every socialist nation in the history of the world. None of them have ever come close to the economic prowess of the countries that have embraced capitalism. Take the example of Communist China and Taiwan. The people living in these two countries are exactly the same, and started at the same level after the Chinese civil war. But communist

THE THREAT

China's economy is socialist, and Taiwan's is capitalist. And over the last 50 years, the people of Taiwan have had a vastly superior economy. Another less stark example is between the United States and Europe. Over the past 20 years, America has enjoyed strong economic growth and very low unemployment. Socialist Europe, on the other hand, has had completely stagnant economies and an average of 10% unemployment—a stark difference indeed. And during President George W. Bush's second term, the United States created more jobs than Europe and Japan combined. The difference between the U.S. and Europe is our economic systems—capitalism vs. socialism. The facts are clear: Capitalism works, and socialism doesn't.

But the facts don't get in the way of the secular-socialists forces. They don't care about the economic success of their nations. They care about power and controlling the lives of others. Capitalism relies on individualism and government getting out of people's way. Socialism directs the economic and social lives of the people and tells them all what to do. And if the secular-socialist forces succeed in their war, these are the people that will be telling us what to do in our lives as well.

America's economic greatness is in large measure a benefit of our individual liberties. Your rights as a citizen not to be infringed upon by the government—in matters of property, the law, taxes, and so on—ensure a stable society in which to operate economically. It is a truism that real economic prosperity is only possible in socially stable societies with legitimate legal systems. The liberties guaranteed to citizens by our Founding Fathers established such a society and legal system. It is also true that private or individual striving and achievement—as opposed to government directed efforts—are far more successful in capitalist societies. So the individualistic nature of our citizenry leads to greater economic advancement, which in turn spurs even more economic growth and advancement. Individuals, unfettered by government shackles, can create an ever-growing economic prosperity in America akin to a snowball rolling down a mountain and turning into an avalanche.

But secular-socialists don't like individualism or personal liberty. Both are dangerous to their plans to control the economy and lives of the citizenry. And so every step of the way, the secular-socialists endeavor to stamp out individualism and liberty. They try to make people more and more dependent on the government (from welfare to government health care to school loans and much, much more). They also do whatever they can to trample the individual rights of citizens in favor of the government. The most recent and egregious example of this is the recent Supreme Court decision that allows government to take people's private property, not for public use as is allowed in the Constitution, but to hand over to others that will pay higher taxes to that government! This outrageous violation of our private property rights is just another battle in the never-ending struggle to chip away at our liberty in America. And it will not stop until the secular-socialists are defeated once and for all.

Both our economic prowess and our individual liberties are derived directly from that fact that America is a Christian nation. It was founded by Christian men, using Christian principles. It credits the source of the rights guaranteed by the Constitution and the Declaration of Independence to a Supreme Being. And as a reward for our Christian foundation, God has made America by far the most blessed nation in the history of the world. American citizens have unprecedented freedom and the opportunity to undertake nearly every endeavor of life for which they are inclined. America's God-given freedom and prosperity is a shining beacon of hope to people around the world. However, our freedom and prosperity—and our Christian heritage itself—are also the source of great hatred by radicals around the globe, and in America itself.

Yes, radical Muslims have declared war against Christian America (discussed later in Section V). But the war on Christian America is not just being fought by militant Muslims around the world. It's also being fought by an equally sinister, and possibly even more deadly, force—one

THE THREAT

within the United States itself. That force is the group of secular-socialist liberal elites in America, who despise our Christian heritage and promote their own Godless version of secular humanism.

In 1962 the liberal Supreme Court took the Bible and prayer out of America's school system. This was the first shot fired in a forty-plus year long war over our religious freedom. A small group of liberal elites—people who don't believe in God and who arrogantly place man over God as the prime mover of events in the universe—are trying to remake the United States in their own image. They do not like the Christian America the Founding Fathers bequeathed to us, and so they are using every weapon in their arsenal to beat religion down so hard that Americans of faith dare not leave their churches.

The America our Founding Fathers bequeathed to us no longer exists. Over the years, elected and appointed officials of this land have slowly but surely chiseled away our rights. Taxes have become oppressively high—as bad as some socialist nations in Europe. Bureaucrats rule our lives. The United Nations has been allowed to dictate our foreign policy. Government agents kill American citizens with barely a peep of protest from the media. And most insidious of all, God and religion are being systematically struck from all aspects of public life. Soon even the tax-exempt status for churches that teach the Bible and fight for your right to freely worship God will be attacked.

These people who are fighting this war against Christian America, those who have foisted their secular doctrines on America, are, simply put, enemies of this nation. They have assaulted our Constitution and our Bill of Rights—and they have nearly destroyed them. If Americans don't do something, and soon, to stop these secular-socialists from destroying Christian America, we will surely witness the destruction of everything that makes the United States great.

War Against Capitalism
★ ★ ★

Capitalism is the greatest economic theory ever invented. It unleashes the creative forces of the human mind, rewards the entrepreneurs for advancing the economy, and has done more to make more people wealthy than any other system in the history of the world. And unlike socialism, it is a moral economic system. The fact that capitalism is a moral economic system is hardly ever mentioned in today's liberal media or classrooms. But it is true. Noted economist Walter E. Williams made this perfectly clear: "*I would identify market efficiency as a side benefit of something far more important. The market talks about moral relationships among individuals. The free market asks us to serve our fellow man in order to have a claim on what he produces. In other words, I serve you by mowing your lawn, and you give me $20. This money is a kind of 'certificate of performance.' I take this evidence of my service to you and go to a grocer and say, 'I demand five pounds of steak that my fellow man produced.' In turn, the grocer says, 'Did you serve your fellow man?' And I say, 'Yes I did, and here are my $20 certificates.' That's the morality of the market. It asks us to serve our fellow man, and the more we serve him the greater the claim we have on what he produces.' Contrast that with governmental immorality. Government can tell me, 'Williams, you can sit on your butt and not mow Father Sirico's lawn. And we will take what he has and give it to you!'*"

The rise of capitalism brought greater morality into our relationships. There is the biblical passage, "*It is as difficult for a rich man to get into Heaven as for a camel to go through the eye of a needle.*" That biblical phrase was quite appropriate for the time because wealth was most often acquired through capturing, plundering and looting your fellow man.

But, with the rise of capitalism, people like Bill Gates are rich because they have served their fellow man. Gates has made his fellow man very happy by building Microsoft computers and software. Fred Smith with Federal Express serves his fellow man, too. The morality of the free market should be stressed because it is far superior to any other method of allocating resources.

The liberal war against capitalism is undermining our economic greatness, and also our nation's morality. Far greater economic experts have already commented on this dire circumstance. For example, the Heritage Foundation, a prominent conservative think tank in Washington, D.C., has made this point clearly as recently as 2006. It said: *"A competitive economy is at the heart of a country's prosperity. Only by producing products or services at or below world prices can countries create wealth. The freedom to access a variety of capital instruments, to hire and fire labor, and to keep the profits of efforts and innovation enhances the economy's potential for growth and wealth creation."*

For many decades, the United States has exemplified this truth, and millions of American families have benefited from America's economic freedom. However, this may change soon. The growing fiscal burden of America's government could hold back the U.S. economy's future by undercutting U.S. competitiveness.

According to the *2006 Index of Economic Freedom*, just published by *The Heritage Foundation* and *The Wall Street Journal*, America's economic freedom ranking has trended down since the Index's inception in 1995. The 161-country survey shows that, even though U.S. economic freedom has improved in absolute terms over the past 12 years, the U.S. has not kept pace with other countries. The degree of improvement has simply not been enough for America to remain one of the top freest economies in the world. Other countries, including Ireland, Estonia, Denmark, and Iceland, have leapfrogged over the United States and now offer greater economic opportunity.

America is still a great place to do business, but a closer examination of the reasons for the slip in its economic freedom ranking shows that

WAKE UP, AMERICA!

America's personal and corporate tax rates are increasingly uncompetitive. For example, many countries throughout Europe have slashed their rates, while the U.S. has done little. If U.S. tax rates do not keep pace with reforms elsewhere, economic growth will be compromised and wealth creation will decline, undermining the government's ability to pay its bills, including its obligations under the Social Security and Medicare programs.

Take a look at nearly every socialist or communist economy in the world. They are basket cases! Socialist France and Germany have over 10% unemployment (America has only 5%). Economic growth is stagnant, or even in decline. And the socialist response to this economic disaster is more and more government programs funded by higher and higher taxes! Look at the example of Japan in the 1990s. From the 1960s through the 1980s, Japan was a model of capitalist success. It emerged from the ashes of World War II to become one of the great economic powers of the world (by many measurements in the 1980s, Japan's economy was even greater than the superpower Soviet Union). But in the late 1980s, Japan's economy took a downturn as a result of a worldwide global recession. The response of the Japanese government to this economic downturn was a massive government spending program. Many analysts at the time hailed this Japanese big government spending program as "investing in its infrastructure" and advised America follow Japan's lead. But what did this vaunted big-government socialist spending program get the Japanese economy? While the United States emerged from recession to have the longest period of peacetime economic growth in American history, the Japanese remained mired in recession. As of the writing of this book, Japan and Europe both remain mired in deep economic trouble, creating fewer jobs combined than the United States alone created in the past six years (and that's even after America suffered the economic devastation of the 9/11 attacks!). But soon, America's economy may not be the envy of the world any longer. As the rate of taxation in America shoots up (compare the tax rate in America from 1900 to today on Figure 1), America comes closer and closer to the socialism that has destroyed the economies of Europe and Japan.

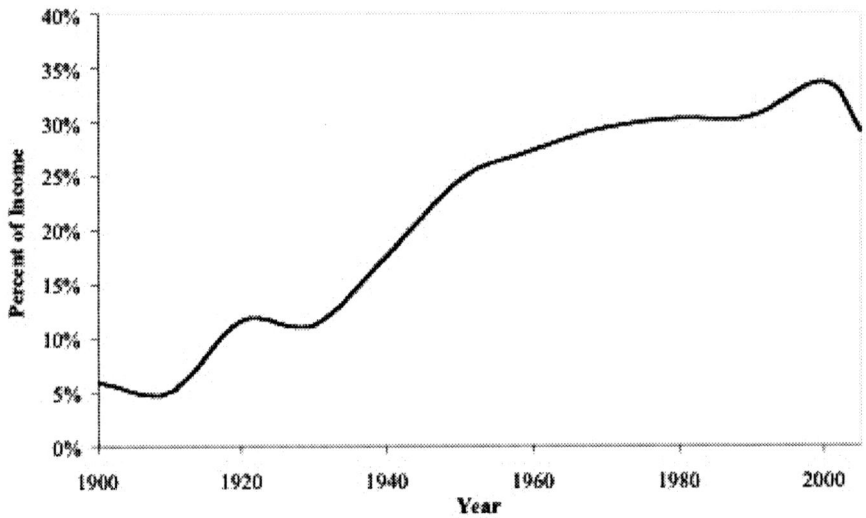

Figure 1. Percentage of Taxed Income.
Source: Tax Foundation

Example after example abound that socialism does not work and hurts the economy. And since capitalism is a moral economic system and socialism is not, the socialist war against capitalism is damaging the moral fiber of America. But as was mentioned before, supporters of socialism and liberalism do not care about economic prosperity for others. They care about accumulating political power for themselves, and don't care how they get it. Socialism and big government gives these liberals the political and economic power to run your life, which is exactly what they want. And they will continue to demonize capitalism at every opportunity. For example, liberal black entertainer Harry Belefonte, who once called President George W. Bush a *"terrorist,"* recently told the crowd at a major black conference during Black History Month that the real enemy of America was capitalism. To this outrageous statement, he was greeted with thunderous applause. And this virulent hatred of capitalism is not limited merely to the liberal black community in America. It extends to virtually every single segment of the liberal and progressive movement in America.

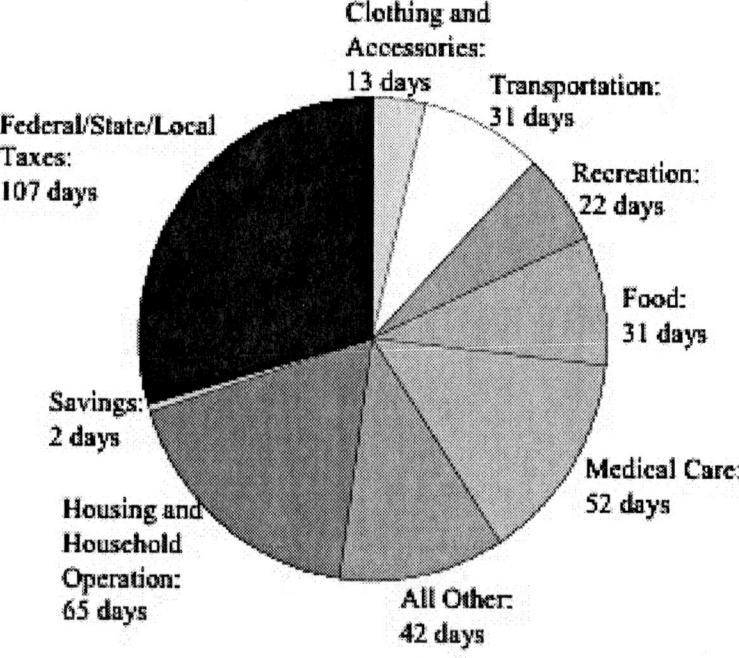

Figure 2. Days Americans Work to Pay Taxes Relative To Other Exp
Source: Tax Foundation Website

If traditional Americans don't wake up to this war against our economic system, which has made so many in our nation so affluent, we will soon face bigger and bigger government control of our lives—and more and more taxes to fund the government behemoth. The accompanying pie chart (Figure 2) illustrates that average Americans work more days a year for the government to pay taxes than for any other expense. And as time goes on, and if trends continue, the government's share of the pie will grow even larger.

War Against Christians

★ ★ ★

The Constitution of the United States is pretty clear about our religious rights. The First Amendment to the Constitution states clearly that: *Congress shall make no law respecting an establishment of religion, or prohibiting the free exercise thereof.*

Despite the relentless efforts of the secular humanists who attack our religious freedoms, this clause of the First Amendment to the Constitution is unequivocal. It states that the United States government can never sponsor or establish any particular religion, to be sure. The First Amendment also established the right of every citizen to freely practice his or her religion in America.

But the true intent of the First Amendment, and the right to freely practice one's religion, has been under assault for the past forty years. And these attacks have ranged from banning children from praying in school to curbing the religious rights of all Americans.

Christians Under Assault

Christians have been under assault for years from the likes of the ACLU and Americans United for the Separation of Church and State. Thanks to these anti-religious radicals and their allies in the judiciary, Christians aren't allowed to display the Ten Commandments, pray in public schools (or even during school events outside of school), or display Nativity scenes in public squares. But at the same time, we are told by the media, school officials, liberal politicians and even some judges that Christians must respect the rights of Muslims to exercise their religious rights in public! This is an outrageous double standard. But it is becoming more and more the norm in America:

WAR AGAINST CHRISTIANS

• Ruth Cline, the Shawnee County, Kansas Treasurer posted an 11 x 14 poster that said, *"In God We Trust"* in her office. This motto is on our coins and dollar bills, but a self-professed pagan filed a complaint against Cline and demanded she *remove* the poster. The ACLU fought the legal battle for the pagan.

• Citizens of Newburyport, Massachusetts who donated money to help refurbish a city park were allowed to have a brick with a personal inscription placed on the sidewalk in the park. One brick said, *"Jesus Loves You,"* and another said, *"For All the Unborn Children."* Both bricks were *removed* by city officials for allegedly violating the separation of church and state.

• Several Colorado legislators campaigned to have prayers *stopped* at the beginning of each legislative day because such prayers are "insensitive."

• Two Cornell legal scholars have recently *protested* the teaching of sexual abstinence in the public schools. They claim it violates the separation of church and state.

• The Fellowship of Christian Athletes were told by Manatee County, Florida school officials they were *banned* from school property even though nonreligious groups were allowed to freely meet.

• In New York City schools, nativity scenes are banned because school officials "did not believe the birth of Jesus was a historical event."

• In Palm Beach, Florida the Muslim Star and Crescent was displayed on public property, but Christian Christmas symbols were *prohibited.*

• The City of Los Angeles *barred* a banner proclaiming *"Jesus is Lord of the High Holidays."*

WAKE UP, AMERICA!

- School officials in Plano, Texas *stopped* a third-grade student from handing out candy canes at Christmas, because the J-shape stood for Jesus.

- An entire New Jersey school district even *outlawed* all Christmas music that mentioned Jesus.

Sadly, these are just a few of the thousands of examples of anti-Christian and anti-religious bigotry. And they are all a direct result of the propaganda spewed by the ACLU and other hate groups against religion and its central role in the formation of our nation.

School Prayer

School prayer has been effectively banned since the Supreme Court - for all intents and purposes—struck prayer from our public schools in 1962.

From the foundation of our nation in 1776 to that disastrous 1962 Supreme Court decision, the United States was a Christian nation. Church attendance was high. Education in America was very often religious. Students prayed and read the Bible daily, even in public schools. And the establishment clause of the First Amendment was never interpreted as prohibiting religion in any state-run institution.

But in the early 1960's, a secular movement began in America to stamp out religion in every corner of the public square. In 1962 the Supreme Court began what was to become a series of disastrous decisions that would obliterate prayer in schools. In the Engel v. Vitale case, the Supreme Court ruled that the creation of an official prayer by the state of New York was unconstitutional. It also ruled that aid to all religions was as equally impermissible as aid to any one religion. Most incomprehensible of all, the Court said that even voluntary prayers by students violated the First Amendment.

Buoyed by their 1962 victory, the opponents of school prayer won another victory in 1963. In Abington School District v. Schempp, the

WAR AGAINST CHRISTIANS

Supreme Court prohibited the then common practice of opening the school day with a prayer or Bible reading. The reasoning behind this decision was that the primary effect of opening the school day with a prayer was the advancement of religion, which according to Engel v. Vitale was now unconstitutional. Never mind that opening the school day with a prayer or a reading of the Bible also advanced the secular goals of promoting morals and good values, the Court said. It advanced religion, and that the Supreme Court would not allow.

Since these disastrous rulings in the early 1960's, the Supreme Court has stood steadfastly by its decision to ban prayer and Bible readings in public schools. The Court even banned a copy of the Ten Commandments in a Kentucky public school, despite its historical, secular importance.

However, the American people have not stood idly by while a few misguided men and women on the Supreme Court tried to strike God and prayer from the public schools. There have been several attempts to pass an amendment to the Constitution which would allow prayer in public schools—despite opposition from the Supreme Court. As Illinois Senator Everett Dirksen said years ago, *"I'm not going to let nine men say to 190 million people, including children, when and where they can utter prayers."* Though none have been successful to date, momentum is shifting toward such an amendment.

There have also been repeated attempts to challenge the conclusions of the Supreme Court's rulings from the state legislatures and the U.S. Congress. Alabama challenged the Court by instituting a "moment of silence" to meditate or pray, but it was later struck down by the Supreme Court in Wallace v. Jaffree. And Congress passed the Equal Access Act in 1984, which said that any school which allows non-religious student groups to meet on school grounds after hours cannot deny religious groups from also meeting on school grounds after hours.

Despite these minor victories, however, the essence of the Supreme

WAKE UP, AMERICA!

Court's opposition to voluntary prayer in public schools has never been reversed—despite the consistent and overwhelming public support for a restoration of prayer to our schools.

In fact, virtually every study since 1962 has demonstrated that the Supreme Court is thwarting the will of the American people on the school prayer issue. From Gallup and Associated Press to NBC and CBS to the New York Times, time after time the polls have shown that around 80%, or four out of every five Americans, support a school prayer amendment. Despite the overwhelming support for school prayer, the Supreme Court has consistently sided with opponents of prayer like the American Civil Liberties Union and has helped drive God and religion from our lives.

America is a Christian nation, socially and historically. Though constituted without an official religion, America is populated largely by Christians and has laws based on Christian tenets and views of the world and the nature of mankind. Since a country's laws inevitably reflect the conscience of its people, America's laws must allow for the religious expression of its people.

It is, therefore, obvious to conclude that the First Amendment was never intended to ban prayer from public schools. Indeed, James Madison himself, who proposed the Amendment, said that, *"he apprehended the meaning of the words to be, that Congress should not establish a religion, and enforce the legal observation of it by law, nor compel men to worship God in any manner contrary to their conscience."*

But whatever the Founding Fathers intended, it doesn't matter to the ACLU and other secular-socialists. Their intent is to destroy the one great institution that stands in their way of complete control and domination of Americans' lives—the God-given individual rights guaranteed to our citizens and the faith in God and His law from which those rights are derived.

War Against Liberty

Our Founding Fathers created a nation and form of government that emphasized personal liberty above all. This emphasis on personal liberty has been a defining aspect of American culture. Because Americans value personal liberty and emphasize individualism so much, we have developed strong leadership and problem-solving capabilities. After all, it's easy to be ruled by others and told what to do with your life. It's hard to make your own decisions and deal with the consequences thereof all on your own.

The positive consequences of the concept of personal liberty in America are enormous. People don't think about this much, but the truth is that the concept of personal liberty is a huge factor in the construction of our law, morality, economic endeavors and life in general. Walter E. Williams summed this notion up incredibly well when he said:

I accept the views of John Locke and David Hume and other philosophers who influenced the Founding Fathers of our country. My core belief is that we all own ourselves. I belong to me and you belong to you. If you believe in self-ownership, certain forms of human behavior are either right or wrong. For example, murder is wrong because it violates private property, that is, my private property, my self-ownership. Rape is wrong. Theft is wrong. If you start with the basic premise of self-ownership, then certain absolutes of necessity follow. If it is wrong for me to take your money by force to give to a poor person, then the same is also wrong for government. I cannot give government any rights that I do not have. I do not have the right to steal from you, so I cannot give government that right either. Natural law under-girds my philosophical view, and I try to conduct my personal life that way.

As you just read, our personal liberty is a crucial aspect of our lives in

America. Our conceptions of right and wrong, our basis of law, and our social constructs are all largely affected by the concept of personal liberty. And this is an excellent thing for us. Without personal liberty, the state (e.g. the government) would have the ability to kill its people at whim, steal from us, and force us to live our lives the way it wanted.

Tragically, this is exactly the type of world that awaits Americans if we allow our government to continue to grow into the socialist behemoth to which it's headed today. As the government continues to grow, it will take more and more from us, both in taxes and in our freedoms. At some point, American citizens will no longer be served by our government. We will be serving it. And on that day when we become slaves to the federal government, we will have lost our personal liberties and our rights to pursue life, liberty and happiness.

Individuals and communities must begin to hold their elected representatives accountable to help slow down this growth of government. One step further, those of us who are Christians need to hold our elected officials to a biblical standard of righteous rule. Only then will local and state governments awaken to the fact that our individual liberties are being usurped by the leviathan of a socialist government bureaucracy. Our elected officials must return to the exercise of their power within the limits established by our Constitution and respective of the individual liberties granted to us by God Himself.

Section III: Who Is Behind It?

When Bill Clinton was first accused of having an affair, Hillary Rodham Clinton went on television to blame this scandal on a "Vast Right-Wing Conspiracy." We all know today that Hillary Clinton's claim of a "Vast Right-Wing Conspiracy" was bunk. She was merely trying to deflect attention away from her husband's infidelity and scandalous behavior. But there really is a Vast Left Wing Conspiracy. And this coalition of secularists, leftists and socialists is working to undermine the United States.

WAKE UP, AMERICA!

Secular humanism is the guiding philosophy behind this Vast Left Wing Conspiracy. Secular humanism seeks to destroy traditional Christian America and turn the United States into a European nation. Secular humanism is based on one important belief: Man, not God, makes the rules in life. Secular humanists want to banish God's rules because they do not care to live in a world of absolute truths. Instead, they want to write the rules of life themselves—essentially live any way they wish.

There are many tools of the secular humanists. The American Civil Liberties Union (ACLU) is one of the more famous. They use the courts to impose their socialist views on the rest of us. The ACLU is closely tied to another tool of secular humanists, liberal judges. These judges override the will of the American people to tyrannically impose their own warped views on the rest of us. Yet another example of a tool of secular humanism is that of the homosexual activists. Since homosexuality is clearly a sin and looked down upon by Christian America, homosexual radicals are doing their best to destroy our religious institutions. If there is no more moral condemnation of homosexuality, these people are free to practice whatever perversions they wish. So a priority of the homosexual agenda is to undermine Christian morality. This also seems to be the goal of many educators in America. Public school officials in the United States have done much to stamp out America's religious heritage by zealously enforcing the ban on prayer and other expressions of religion. As a result, we are raising a generation of Americans who know nothing of the vital importance of our religious heritage. And this is exactly what the secular humanists want.

Another less obvious, but just as dangerous, tool of secular humanism comes from without. It is that of International Socialism and the United Nations. Most of the world is run by either socialists or plain old dictators. The rulers of these countries cannot stand the example of the United States—our freedom and our prosperity—because it makes them look bad. If given a choice, most people in the rest of the world would live as Americans do! But they often aren't given a choice in the socialist governments or dictatorships in which they live. That can lead to great social unrest with the people of these countries. So what many other governments in the world do is try to undermine the United States and our values, to make it look far less attractive to their own people. And these governments often use the United Nations to advance their anti-American and pro-socialist agenda. Their ultimate goal is to undermine our Christian heritage, strip away our liberties, and impose socialism on our economy to bring the United States down to the level of the rest of the world. That way, without the example of American greatness to inspire people around the globe, these foreign rulers don't have to worry about revolution in their own countries nearly as much.

There can be no doubt, America's traditional institutions are under brutal assault, both from forces without and from within our nation.

Section III: Who is Behind It?

Secular Humanism

★ ★ ★

Secular humanism—the guiding philosophy that currently rules Europe and which is gaining ever more ground in America—is based on one important belief: Man, not God, makes the rules in life. Secular humanists want to banish God's rules, because they do not care to live in a world of absolute truths. Instead, they want to write the rules of life themselves—essentially live any way they wish. Tragically, as we have seen in every manifestation of secular humanism, this has led to nothing but tyranny and misery and suffering for those who toil under its yoke. When man gets to make the rules up on his own with his finite power and intellect, he invariably rules as a tyrant. When man rules as a tyrant, the people living under that system suffer. It's a constant theme seen throughout history. On the other hand, when man follows God's rules, the nation and the people flourish because they adhere to universal truths.

Secular humanism is the guiding philosophy behind those seeking to destroy traditional Christian America and turn it into a European nation. The founding document of the secular humanism movement is *The Humanist Manifesto*, first published in the 1930s. In 1973, an updated edition called *The Humanist Manifesto II* was published,. Here are the five basic tenets of humanism, based on *The Human Manifesto II*:

Tenet I: Atheism

"Religious humanists regard the universe as self-existing and not created. We find insufficient evidence for belief in the existence of a supernatural; it is either meaningless or irrelevant to the question of the survival and fulfillment of the human race. As nontheists, we begin with humans, not God, not nature, not deity. Nature may indeed be broader and deeper than we now know; any new discoveries, however, will but enlarge our knowledge of the natural...but we can discover no divine purpose or providence for the human species. While there is much that we do not know, humans are responsible for what we are or will become. No deity will save us, we must save ourselves."

Tenet II: Evolution

"Humanism believes that man is a part of nature and that he has emerged as a result of continuous process...Holding an organic view of life, humanists find that the traditional dualism of mind and body must be rejected...Humanism recognized that man's religious culture and civilization, as clearly depicted by anthropology and history, are the product of gradual development due to his interaction with his environment and with his social heritage. The individual born into a particular culture is largely molded to that culture...science affirms that the human species is an emergence from natural evolutionary forces. As far as we know, the total personality is a function of the biological organism transacting in a social and cultural contest."

Tenet III: Amorality

"We affirm that moral values derive their source from human experience. Ethics is autonomous and situational, needing no theological or ideological sanction. Ethics stem from human need and interest. To deny this distorts the whole basis of life. In the area of sexuality, we believe that intolerant attitudes, often cultivated by orthodox religions and puritanical cultures, unduly repress sexual conduct. The right to birth control, abortion, and divorce should be recognized. While we do not approve of exploitative, denigration forms of sexual expression, neither do we wish to prohibit, by law or social sanction, sexual behavior between consenting adults. The many varieties of sexual exploration should not in themselves be considered 'evil.' Without countenancing mindless permissiveness or unbridled promiscuity, a civilized society should be a tolerant one. Short of harming others or compelling them to do likewise, individuals should be permitted to express their sexual proclivities and pursue their life-styles as they desire. We wish to cultivate the development of a responsible attitude toward sexuality, in which humans are not exploited as sexual objects, and in which intimacy, sensitivity, respect, and honesty in interpersonal relations are encouraged. Moral education for children and adults is an important way of developing awareness and sexual maturity."

Tenet IV: Individual Autonomy

"Human life has meaning because we create and develop our futures. Happiness and creative realization of human need and desires, individually and in shared enjoyment, are continuous themes in humanism. We strive for the good life, here and now. The goal is to pursue life's enrichment despite debasing forces of vulgarization, commercialization, bureaucratization, and dehumanization...Reason and intelligence are the most effective instruments that humankind possesses. There is no substitute; neither faith nor passion suffices in itself. The controlled use of scientific methods, which have transformed the natural and social sciences since the Renaissance, must be extended further in the solution of human problems...To enhance freedom and dignity the individual must experience a full range of civil liberties in all societies. This included freedom of speech and the press, fair judicial process, religious liberty, freedom of association, and artistic, scientific, and cultural freedom. It also includes a recognition of an individual's right to die with dignity, euthanasia, and the right to suicide.

We oppose the increasing invasion of privacy, by whatever means, in both totalitarian and democratic societies. We would safeguard, extend, and implement the principle of human freedom evolved from the Magna Carta to the Bill of Rights, the Rights of Man, and the Universal Declaration of Human Rights...The preciousness and dignity of the individual person is a central humanist value. Individuals should be encouraged to realize their own creative talents and desires. We reject all religious, ideological, or moral codes that denigrate the individual, suppress freedom, dull intellect, dehumanize personality. We believe in maximum individual autonomy consonant with social responsibility. Although science can account for the causes of behavior, the possibilities of individual freedom of choice exist in human life and should be increased."

Tenet V: Socialistic One-World View
"We deplore the division of humankind on nationalistic grounds. We have reached a turning point in human history where the best option is to transcend the limits of national sovereignty and to move toward the building of a world community in which all sectors of the human family can participate. Thus we look to the development of a system of world law and a world order based upon transnational federal government. This would appreciate cultural pluralism and diversity. It would not exclude pride in national origins and accomplishments nor the handling of regional problems on a regional basis. Human progress, however, can no longer be achieved by focusing on one section of the world, Western or Eastern, developed or underdeveloped. For the first time in human history, no part of human kind can be isolated from any other. Each person's future is in some way linked to all. We thus reaffirm a commitment to the building of world community, at the same time recognizing that this commits us to some hard choices…the problem of economic growth and development can no longer be resolved by one nation alone; they are worldwide in scope. It is the moral obligation of the developed nations to provide—through an international authority that safeguards human rights—massive technical, agricultural, medical, and economic assistance, including birth control techniques, to the developing portions of the globe. World poverty must cease. Hence extreme disproportions in wealth, income, and eco-

nomic growth should be reduced on a worldwide basis.

The principle of moral equality must be furthered through elimination of all discrimination based upon race, religion, sex, age, or national origin. This means equality of opportunity and recognition of talent and merit. Individuals should be encouraged to contribute to their own betterment. If unable, then society should provide means to satisfy their basic economic, health, and cultural needs, including, wherever resources make possible, a minimum guaranteed annual income."

These tenets are for all intents and purposes a repudiation of God and his laws! And for the past forty-plus years, these tenets have slowly crept into our society's laws. As a result, we've seen a devastating decline in lawfulness, morality and decency in our nation. In essence, secular humanism is destroying the moral fabric of America and turning our nation into a socialist European state.

Tools of the Secular Humanists: The A.C.L.U.

The ACLU was founded in 1920 by Roger Baldwin, for the purposes of "defending" the "rights" of citizens from the "totalitarian" American government.

Baldwin, a proponent of the Human Manifesto and secular humanism, knew exactly how he was going to attack America and our institutions. The following quote is a revealing insight regarding exactly how the ACLU has gone about achieving their goals. In order to achieve their goals Baldwin said, *"The courts are the vehicles we use to assert our interpretation of the US Constitution."* This statement reveals an admission that the ACLU's view of our own Constitution is a different interpretation than the view held by most Americans. It also reveals the ACLU is attacking America from the inside by using our very own courts and governmental systems.

Does this sound familiar? Former Soviet ruler Nikita Khruschev once said, *"We will bury you!"* When asked if he was saying that Russia would destroy us militarily, he said, *"No, we will destroy you from the inside out."*

Soviet Communism failed to destroy America. But today, an enemy of freedom has infiltrated our nation, hijacked our own planes and used them as weapons against our own institutions. These terrorists claim that they are defending our freedom. But in truth they are destroying our freedom and the institutions that protect American liberty. This internal terrorist group is the ACLU.

James Madison, known to be the Architect of our Constitution said, *"We have staked the whole future of American civilization, not upon the power of government, far from it. We have staked the future of all of our political institutions upon the capacity of mankind for self government; upon*

TOOLS OF THE SECULAR HUMANISTS: THE A.C.L.U.

the capacity of each and all of us to govern ourselves, to control ourselves, to sustain ourselves according to the Ten Commandments of God."

French statesman Alexis de Tocqueville, who studied America at great length in an attempt to determine what made America great said, "*America is great because America is good, and if America ever ceases to be good, America will cease to be great.*" Clearly, both men believed that America's greatness derived from our great morality and belief in God. But the ACLU does not believe this to be true. In fact, the ACLU has done everything in its power to destroy the very religious institutions upon which America's freedom and greatness are derived.

The well-funded American Civil Liberties Union is at the vanguard of the secular humanist army that is waging war against religious freedom. And the ACLU makes no bones about its opposition to religion. For example, the ACLU's national board policy #81(a) states in part:

The ACLU believes that any program of religious indoctrination—direct or indirect—in the public schools or by use of public resources is a violation of the constitutional principle of separation of church and state and must be opposed.

The policy further states that the ACLU:

…opposes the infusion of other types of religious practices and standards into the public schools. These include such practices as baccalaureate exercises in the form of religious services, prayer meetings at athletic events, the taking of religious census of pupils…and the profession of religious observance or belief as a consideration in the evaluation and promotion of teachers.

The ACLU contends that public schools that allow religion would "indoctrinate impressionable young people into an officially endorsed religion. What is tyranny, if not that?"

Tyranny? The ACLU is actually calling the exercise of religious freedom tyranny. If anyone is being a tyrant, it is the ACLU itself for denying American citizens their constitutionally-guaranteed rights.

WAKE UP, AMERICA!

And the cornerstone of the ACLU's campaign to abolish religion from American life once and for all is their massive misinformation campaign.

Just read the following mean-spirited excerpts from a pamphlet published by the Freedom From Religion Foundation, a key ACLU ally:

When religion has invaded our public school system, it has singled out the lone Jewish student, the class Unitarian or agnostic, the children in the minority. Families who protest state/church violations in our public schools invariably experience persecution. It was commonplace prior to the court decisions against school prayer to put nonreligious or nonorthodox children in places of detention during bible-reading or prayer recitation. The children of Supreme Court plaintiffs against religion in schools, such as Vashti McCollum, Ed Schempp and Ishmael Jaffree, were beaten up on the way to and from school, their families subjected to community harassment and death threats for speaking out in defense of a constitutional principle. We know from history how harmful and destructive religion is in our public schools. In those school districts that do not abide by the law, school children continue to be persecuted today.

This group talks about children and families being "persecuted." But who are the persecuted ones here? Are they the one or two children who may have been ostracized by private citizens for their beliefs? Or are they the vast majority of children and families who are prevented from exercising their right to pray by the United States government? The answer is clear. The pamphlet goes on:

Proponents of the so-called 'voluntary' school prayer amendment are admitting that our secular Constitution prohibits organized prayers in public schools. Otherwise, why would an amendment to our U.S. Constitution be required? The nation must ask whether politically motivated Newt Gingrich & Co. are wiser than James Madison, principle author of the Constitution, and the other founders who engineered the world's oldest and most successful constitution! The radical school prayer amendment would negate the First Amendment's guarantee against gov-

TOOLS OF THE SECULAR HUMANISTS: THE A.C.L.U.

ernment establishment of religion. Most distressing, it would be at the expense of the civil rights of children, America's most vulnerable class. It would attack the heart of the Bill of Rights, which safeguards the rights of individuals from the tyranny of the majority.

There are too many untruths and mis-statements in the previous paragraph to rebut them all. But even they must know that no one who supports a school prayer amendment is stating that the Constitution already bans prayer in school. An amendment to the Constitution has become necessary because the Supreme Court, at the behest of the ACLU, has hijacked the First Amendment and denied our religious freedom. And if you have any doubt of that, the pamphlet continues:

Student-Initiated Prayer is a ruse proposed by extremist Christian legal groups. Religious coercion is even worse at the hands of another student, subjecting students to peer pressure, pitting students in the majority against students in the minority, treating them as outsiders with school complicity. Imposing prayer-by-majority-vote is flagrant and insensitive abuse of school authority. Such schools should be teaching students about the purpose of the Bill of Rights, instead of teaching them to be religious bullies. Some principals or school boards even have made seniors hold open class votes on whether to pray at graduation, leading to hostility and reprisal against those students brave enough to stand up for the First Amendment.

Based on these writings, one can conclude that the ACLU's war against religious freedom is based on nothing other than an irrational and hateful opposition to God and faith. As a result, we see their never-ending legal war to erode each and every religious liberty granted to Americans by God and protected by our Constitution. The ACLU has already won many major legal battles in this war, and expects to win many more. Each ACLU victory brings them closer to their goal of a religion-free zone in America, and brings the United States closer to that socialist and secular type of society we see in Europe today.

Tools of the Secular Humanists: Judges

★ ★ ★

Today, Americans live under what Judge Robert Bork has rightly called "Our Judicial Oligarchy." Judge Bork states that the U.S. Supreme Court Justices "are our masters in a way that no President, Congressman, governor, or other elected official is. They order our lives and we have no recourse, no means of resisting, no means of altering their ukases. They are indeed robed masters." (Robert Bork, "Our Judicial Oligarchy," First Things, November, 1996, pgs 21-24) And this judicial tyranny does not stop at the Supreme Court. Lower federal court judges are just as guilty of imposing their own views on our lives. In short, our nation is not governed by a written Constitution or by laws passed by the U.S. Congress or state legislatures. We are ruled by a handful of unelected judges who act as our robed masters.

These liberal judges have banned prayer in our children's schools and Bibles from teachers' desks (even though these teachers only read their Bibles to themselves on lunch breaks!). These judicial tyrants have also imposed their dictates on the American people in the realms of abortion, marriage, adoption, sodomy, and much more. Far too often these judicial rulings have turned traditional values on its head, which has led directly to the tearing of America's moral fabric. Perhaps the greatest threat to America today is out-of-control judicial tyrants who are imposing their own warped views on the rest of us and ruining our country.

One of the most egregious cases of liberal judicial tyranny is the battle over the Ten Commandments. For 200 years, Americans have had the right to display this most sacred Christian symbol in public in homage to its key role in developing both our morality and our law. But last year, the U.S. Supreme Court issued two decisions on the public display of the

TOOLS OF THE SECULAR HUMANISTS: JUDGES

Ten Commandments. One case involved the framed display of the Ten Commandments on the walls of courthouses in Kentucky. The other case involved a Ten Commandments monument on display on government property in Texas. In the Kentucky case, the court ruled 5-4 that the framed copies of the Ten Commandments implied an endorsement of religion and were unconstitutional. In the Texas decision, the court ruled that the Ten Commandments monument on the grounds of the state capitol served a secular purpose and was thus legal.

These two decisions show how confused the court is over the issue of religious freedom and the public display of religious symbols. Supreme Court Justice Antonin Scalia, writing his dissent from the court on the Kentucky case, said: *What distinguishes the rule of law from the dictatorship of a shifting Supreme Court majority is the absolutely indispensable requirement that judicial opinions be grounded in consistently applied principle. That is what prevents judges from ruling now this way, now that—thumbs up or thumbs down—as their personal preferences dictate. Today's opinion forthrightly (or actually, somewhat less than forthrightly) admits that it does not rest upon consistently applied principle.*

This is just one of many examples of judicial tyranny oppressing the rights of the American people. And there are many more examples of judicial tyranny. Here are just a few:

- The federal 9th Circuit Court of Appeals in San Francisco ruled in favor of atheist Michael Newdow that the words, *"One nation, under God"* in the Pledge of Allegiance were unconstitutional. The ruling was handed down by a three-judge panel with only two judges deciding the case. (The Supreme Court threw out this case on a technicality, but as of the writing of this book it was working its way back to the Supreme Court.)

- Florida Circuit Judge Gerard O'Brien ruled that a female-to-male transgender is legally a man under state law and can adopt her ex-wife's teenage son. According to Judge O'Brien, sex is determined by your mind, not by genetics or your DNA. In this decision, O'Brien has declared that maleness and femaleness are simply matters of opinion—not biological facts. According to lawyers involved in this battle, O'Brien's bizarre ruling, "*could really undermine all objectivity within the legal system, and we believe that it has great importance to not only the legal system, but also to marriage and to many other classifications that we recognized as protected statuses, such as national origin or race and many others,*". ("Transgender Cases Focuses on How Sex is Determined," CNSNews.com, July 24, 2003)

Judge O'Brien is a judicial tyrant who has ignored genetics and biological facts in making his ruling on gender and sex.

• The U.S. Supreme Court by a vote of 6-3 overturned laws against homosexual sodomy in 14 states. In other words, six lawyers in black robes overturned the will of millions of American citizens with the stroke of a pen. And as is the case with so many other liberal judicial rulings, this decision will have terrible and far-reaching effects. According to Justice Antonin Scalia in his dissent, the Court's decision now calls into question state laws against bigamy, same-sex marriage, adult incest, prostitution, masturbation, adultery, fornication, bestiality, and obscenity! Scalia notes that the U.S. Supreme Court, "*...has largely signed on to the so-called homosexual agenda, by which I mean the agenda promoted by some homosexual activists directed at eliminating the moral opprobrium that has traditionally attached to homosexual conduct.*"

• In 1973, the U.S. Supreme Court "discovered" a "right" within the Constitution that had remained hidden for nearly two centuries since our nation's founding: The "right" of women to kill their unborn children. This "right" was created by the late Justice Harry Blackmun, who discovered what he described as a "penumbra" (or shadow) of privacy rights in

TOOLS OF THE SECULAR HUMANISTS: JUDGES

the 14th Amendment to the Constitution. This penumbra of privacy rights included the "right" of a woman to kill her unborn baby on demand. Because of this most terrible of all the examples of judicial tyranny, more than 30 million babies have died since 1973.

Judges have usurped much power rightfully vested in our executive and legislative branches of government. Both the President and Congress are partially at fault for allowing this usurpation of power to occur. Apathetic Americans who refuse to rise up in opposition to this judicial usurpation of power are also partially at fault. But the group most to blame for this judicial disaster are the liberal secular humanists.

Liberals have seen that they are incapable of winning their agenda via the ballot box. When undisguised liberal policies or politicians are put up for a vote on a national level, they nearly invariably lose. And liberals are aware that their policies are unpopular with the American people. But they have devised a plan to enact their agenda anyway — the court system. Liberals have focused a great deal of energy ensuring that they pack the courts with similar-thinking secular humanists. No more evidence of this is needed than an examination of the action of Senate Democrats in regards to President George W. Bush's judicial nominees. Senate Democrats did everything in their power, including filibusters, to prevent President Bush from replacing their precious liberal judges with conservative nominees. These Senate Democrats knew that if President Bush's nominees got to the bench, their last chance to implement their agenda would be lost.

The battle over the judiciary in the near future is going to be one of the most important battles for the soul of America. If traditionalists are successful, the judiciary will return to the role the Founding Fathers intended for it—interpreting laws rather than making up their own laws. If liberal secular humanists succeed in this battle, America will become an irreligious socialist country in the model of socialist Europe, ruled by tyrant bureaucrats in black robes.

WAKE UP, AMERICA!

The Myth of Separation

Clearly, the danger to America posed by liberal secular judges is dire. They threaten to dismantle each and every founding institution bequeathed to us by our Founding Fathers. No more stark example of this can be seen than the example of liberal judges warping the original meaning of separation of church and state.

Possibly the most misunderstood phrase in regards to our constitutional rights is separation of church and state. In fact, the very phrase cannot be found anywhere in our Preamble, Constitution, Bill of Rights, Declaration of Independence or any other official document of the United States. It was brought into being by a judge on the Supreme Court.

A number of anti-Christian groups, such as the ACLU, have repeatedly used this judge's assertion to claim that separation of church and state is the law of the land. Today, many believe that the "law" of separation of church and state is real. IT IS NOT.

Others believe that we have a law of separation of church and state in the First Amendment of the Constitution. WE DO NOT. The so-called "law" of separation of church and state just simply does not exist even though people often repeat that it does.

We have all heard media reports that say you can't publicly display the Ten Commandments, nor any other sign of your Christian faith, because of the "law" of separation of church and state. There is no such law on the books anywhere in America. The "law" of separation has become widely accepted as truth because of a misunderstanding about the wording and a twisted ACLU argument about the original intent of the First Amendment. But liberal courts have given credence to this "new," albeit incorrect, interpretation of the First Amendment.

From the ratification of the First Amendment and for more than 170 years following the adoption of the First Amendment, the phrase *"separation of church and state"* was never mentioned in connection with the First Amendment. Today, the phrase *"separation of church and state"* is

TOOLS OF THE SECULAR HUMANISTS: JUDGES

often mentioned, incorrectly, in the same breath as the First Amendment. The argument is simply disingenuous.

During the years when the First Amendment was interpreted literally, none of today's court cases which attack Christianity would have stood a chance. In fact, although there were a few cases that dealt with religious freedom before the 1960s, they were dealt with firmly by judges who interpreted the Constitution literally, exactly as it was written.

Remember what is restricted by this Amendment—the government. In America, people are still free to make their own choices. This amendment does not place any limitation upon citizens, collectively or individually. Therefore, it is the people who are being protected against the power of our government.

All this changed suddenly in 1962, when the anti-Christian ACLU convinced our Supreme Court that the First Amendment meant something altogether different than was ever intended by our Christian patriotic founders.

Today the First Amendment plays a significant role in lawsuits involving religion, but that has not always been true. In the 1962 case of *Engle v. Vitale*, the ACLU was able to convince the Supreme Court that the First Amendment meant something that no other court had ever said before. The ACLU's perverted misinterpretation of the First Amendment became responsible for today's myriad of new and frivolous lawsuits. The purpose of these lawsuits is to attack Christianity in America and remove every trace of God from public view in America.

Since our Founding Fathers were Christians, freedom of religion meant the freedom to exercise the *religion of your chosen denomination*. Any other interpretation or argument is without the support of any historical fact, and without any reasonable foundation.

The freedom of religion, free speech, freedom of press and the right to peaceably assemble were obviously the top priorities for our founders. Therefore, they addressed these issues in the First Amendment. Freedom

WAKE UP, AMERICA!

of religion was first in the First Amendment, not the 200th amendment.

When we read about court cases that involve questions of school prayer, hanging the Ten Commandments in public places, or allowing nativity scenes, or other "religious" displays, it is the phrase of the First Amendment that is frequently called the "establishment clause" which is referred to in newspaper articles reporting these cases. We frequently read that the ACLU is contending that a public display of the Ten Commandments is a violation of the "establishment clause" and is therefore unconstitutional. Obviously they are reading from a different book.

The First Amendment guarantees freedom of religion. Although our founders were thinking of freedom for each denomination, because they were all Christians, today the ACLU has convinced our courts that the First Amendment means *freedom from religion*. But how in the world did they ever do that?

The ACLU convinced the court that the words religion or denomination really meant Christianity (Notice that Christianity is at the center of the ACLU's attack.). Then the ACLU said that the word Congress did not mean Congress. Instead, the ACLU said that the word congress supposedly meant any tax supported organization such as a school, courthouse or library. Next they said that any action like displaying the Ten Commandments by any tax-supported organization (e.g., schools, courthouses, or libraries) was exactly the same as if it had been done by the Congress. And lastly they argued that if a courthouse hung the Ten Commandments it was exactly the same as if *congress passed a law that represented the establishment of religion.*

This is an outrage and is unbelievably mind-boggling. There is no truth in this argument and it is clear that the victims of this atrocity are America's people of faith.

In 1962, the ACLU claimed its first victims. The U.S. Supreme Court decided that if elementary school children were allowed to say a morning prayer, they were doing the same thing as if Congress passed a law estab-

TOOLS OF THE SECULAR HUMANISTS: JUDGES

lishing one denomination as our national denomination. It was quite remarkable that when it became time for the Supreme Court to site the precedents upon which this decision was based, they were not able to cite even one precedent. But that was because there were none. They had no former court case that ever ruled this way, and they had to look *outside of all prior cases ever ruled upon by the supreme court for a reason to explain their action!* After searching for something to hang their hats upon, they came up with the phrase *"separation of church and state."*

The phrase *"separation of church and state"* is nowhere to be found in our Declaration of Independence, Constitution, First Amendment, nor any other official document of the United States government. It was coined by Thomas Jefferson in a personal letter he wrote to a group of Baptists in Danbury, Connecticut. They had asked if there was to be a national denomination and Jefferson wrote back to assure them that this would never happen because of the First Amendment had created a wall of separation of church and state.

The ACLU and other anti-Christian organizations love to talk about the law of separation of church and state. They gleefully point to the "law" mentioned in Thomas Jefferson's letter. However, they fail to quote Jefferson when he said, *"No power over the freedom of religion is given to the United States, by the Constitution."* It is also interesting to note that when the Bill of Rights was written, Thomas Jefferson played no role in drafting the documents. He was not in the country at the time.

For Christians, the separation of church and state is not only a flawed legal argument, but it is also an ungodly principle. First, it is nearly impossible to separate people from anything they have chosen to believe and is a part of their very make-up. If a man has high ideals and they are a part of him, how can you separate him from those ideals and expect him to not allow his deep-rooted thoughts and values to accompany him to school, work or the grocery store? The state (e.g. the government) is made up of men and women. Does God want to separate men and women (the state) from the church? The answer is clearly no.

The ACLU argued that the establishment clause ("Congress shall enact no law regarding the establishment of religion") meant that if a tax supported courthouse displays the Ten Commandments, that action is exactly the same as if Congress enacted a law and was establishing a religion—in this case, Christianity. And that, according to the ACLU's version of the First Amendment establishment clause, was prohibited and therefore unconstitutional.

The literal interpretation of the establishment clause should lead the court to ask a simple question: Did Congress enact any law that established a religion? The answer is clearly, no, they did not. Case dismissed!

Not only is that clear from the deep researching of the times, but since there were only Christians of different denominations in America at the time, the Founding Fathers obviously were not thinking about Buddhists in Japan who were literally a world away. When Americans allowed the ACLU to deny the literal interpretation of our Constitution, we gave up the principles of our founders, the principles of our Christian Heritage, and the principles that soldiers in two world wars fought to defend.

As a result of the ACLU's relentless attack upon Christianity and morality, we have seen a huge change in our nation. Since 1962, divorce rates, teenage pregnancies and violent crimes have skyrocketed. Too many Americans no longer uphold truth, honesty and morality. Instead, for many Americans, decadence and self-absorption rule the day.

The rules of society that created this great nation have now given way to a society where there are no rules. And this has brought us to the deprivation we find our nation in today.

Prior to the liberal judiciary's twisted series of attacks upon the very moral fiber of America, we were a nation that played by the rules and respected one another. We understood that freedom and success came from operating within the guidelines of generally accepted principles. Somehow those ideas have been replaced with the idea that freedom

TOOLS OF THE SECULAR HUMANISTS: JUDGES

comes only when you have no rules. If it feels good, do it. Instant gratification seems to be more important than someone else's well being, or even more important than the consequences you yourself may face. As a result, we now have school shootings, metal detectors in public buildings, "hooking up," drug sniffing dogs, drive-by shootings, abortion upon demand, no-fault divorce, condoms handed out by public schools to teenagers without their parents' consent, and homosexual propaganda being taught to our children in elementary schools.

Tools of the Secular Humanists: Educators

★ ★ ★

As has been discussed, the First Amendment says that the United States government should never sponsor or establish any particular religion. And it should also never stop a citizen from practicing his or her religion. But the exact opposite has happened in our public schools in the matter of prayer.

From the time our country was founded until that fateful Supreme Court decision, education in the United States was often religious. Students prayed and read the Bible daily, even in public schools. And the establishment clause of the First Amendment was never interpreted as prohibiting religion in any state-run institution.

In 1962 the Supreme Court began what was to become a series of disastrous decisions against prayer in schools. In the *Engel v. Vitale* case, the Court ruled that the formation of an official prayer by the state of New York was unconstitutional and that aid to all religions was as impermissible as aid to any one religion. Most incomprehensibly of all, the Court said that even voluntary prayers by students violated the First Amendment.

Buoyed by their 1962 victory, the opponents of school prayer won another victory in 1963. In the *Abington School District v. Schempp*, the Supreme Court prohibited the then-common practice of opening the school day with a prayer or Bible reading. The reason for its decision was that the primary effect of opening the school day with a prayer was the advancement of religion, which according to *Engel v. Vitale* was now unconstitutional. Never mind that opening the school day with a prayer or a reading of the Bible also advanced the secular goals of promoting morals and good values, the Court said. It advanced religion, and that the Supreme Court would not allow.

TOOLS OF THE SECULAR HUMANISTS: EDUCATORS

Since these disastrous rulings in the early 1960s, the Supreme Court has stood steadfastly by its decision to ban prayer and Bible readings in public schools. It even banned a copy of the Ten Commandments in a Kentucky public school, despite its historical, secular importance.

That does not mean that the American people have stood idly by while a few misguided men and women on the Supreme Court tried to strike God and prayer from the public schools. There have been several attempts to pass an amendment to the Constitution that would allow prayer in public schools—despite opposition from the Supreme Court. As Illinois Senator Everett Dirksen said years ago, *"I'm not going to let nine men say to 190 million people, including children, when and where they can utter prayers."* Though none have been successful to date, momentum is shifting toward such an amendment.

There have also been repeated attempts to challenge the conclusions of the Supreme Court's rulings from the state legislatures and the U.S. Congress. Alabama challenged the Court by instituting a "moment of silence" to meditate or pray, but it was later struck down by the Supreme Court in Wallace v. Jaffree. And Congress passed the Equal Access Act in 1984, which said that any school which allows non-religious student groups to meet on school grounds after hours cannot deny religious groups from also meeting on school grounds after hours.

Despite these minor victories, however, the essence of the Supreme Court's opposition to voluntary prayer in public schools has never been reversed—even though there remained a consistent and overwhelming public support for a restoration of prayer to our schools.

In fact, virtually every study since 1962 has demonstrated that the Supreme Court is thwarting the will of the American people on the school prayer issue. From Gallup and Associated Press to NBC and CBS to the New York Times, time after time the polls have shown that around 80%, or four out of every five Americans, support a school prayer amendment. Despite the overwhelming support for school prayer, the

WAKE UP, AMERICA!

Supreme Court has consistently sided with opponents of prayer, like the American Civil Liberties Union, and has helped drive God and religion from our lives.

Many educators in America seem to be gleefully going along with this war against prayer and religion in school. Here are just a few of the hundreds of examples compiled by Congressman Ernest Istook, a strong proponent of religious freedom in Congress, of how educators have trampled religious liberty in our schools:

• A principle in a Virginia public school **barred a young girl from reading the Bible** on the school bus.

• A Christian minister was **forbidden** by a federal judge from speaking to public school children in Texas about the dangers of drugs simply because he was a man of God.

• In Alaska public school students were **prohibited from using the word "Christmas"** because the word "Christ" was in it.

• A high school valedictorian in Hawaii was told by her principle that she **violated Department of Education policy** by thanking God in her graduation speech.

• In Missouri an elementary school student was **placed in a week-long detention** for bowing his head over his lunch in prayer.

This bureaucratic assault on the rights of our citizens by the educators in America cannot be tolerated any longer. If the secular humanists succeed in indoctrinating our children in their schools, the next generation will be completely without the understanding of our country's Christian heritage and the importance religion and faith have to the success of our nation.

Tools of the Secular Humanists: Homosexual Activists

★ ★ ★

As was mentioned, homosexual activists are desperately trying to "normalize" their sinful behavior in our society. Since homosexuality is clearly a sin and looked down upon by Christian America, homosexual radicals are doing their level best to destroy our religious institutions. If there is no more moral condemnation of homosexuality, these people are free to practice whatever perversions they wish.

In a book review of *The Homosexual Agenda* by Alan Sears and Craig Osten, reviewer Sandra Alexander makes it clear exactly what the homosexual radicals want: In the introduction to their book, *The Homosexual Agenda, Mr. Sears and Mr. Osten ask the question, "How far down the road have homosexual activists taken us toward their goal of unbridled sexual behavior and silencing of the church?" (p. 14) They then describe the four stages which lead to the moral demise of a culture, stating that the homosexuals, after quickly passing through the first two stages, are now finishing the third stage ('The Mobilization Stage'), developing a common language and strategy for presenting their case to the public.*

They [homosexual advocates] reframed the issue, taking it out of the moral realm, and presented it as a 'human rights' issue. Those who opposed their argument were deemed 'hateful' or 'intolerant' toward those that are 'different'—even though the group's only identification is that of a chosen sexual behavior." (p. 14) This strategy is working, because "once an issue has been redefined from a moral absolute to an individual choice, society starts to be reprogrammed that the arguments of the group are valid and therefore special privileges for previous 'injustices' and for the affirmation of the behavior occur." This is stage four, "The Legitimization Stage." (p. 14) The authors warn us that we have now reached stage four and they ask the question,

TOOLS OF THE SECULAR HUMANISTS: HOMOSEXUAL ACTIVISTS

"How has one to two percent of the population achieved so much success in transforming American culture and restricting religious freedom?" (p. 17)

Part of the answer to the question is found in two publications (1987 and 1989) by homosexual activists Marshall Kirk and Hunter Madsen. Their strategy to change America's perception of homosexual behavior included the following six points:

1. *Talk about gays and gayness as loudly and often as possible.* (Through sheer perseverance the opposition will be worn down)

2. *Portray gays as victims, not aggressive challengers.*

3. *Give homosexual protectors a "just" cause.*

4. *Make gays look good.* (Notice that the media always makes the gay character the hero)

5. *Make the victimizers look bad.*

6. *Solicit funds: the buck stops here* (i.e., get corporate America and major foundations to financially support the homosexual cause). (p. 18)

Kirk and Madsen knew that Bible-believing Christians would be the major opponents of legitimizing homosexuality because of their belief in the Biblical teaching that homosexuality is "unnatural" and "vile." To counteract this, they stated, "We can undermine the moral authority of homophobic churches by portraying them as antiquated backwaters, badly out of step with the times and with the latest findings of psychology. Against the mighty pull of institutional religion, one must set the mightier draw of science and public opinion....Such an unholy alliance has worked well against churches before, on such topics as divorce and abortion." (p. 20) In addition to this Kirk and Madsen wrote, "We intend to make the antigays look so nasty that average

WAKE UP, AMERICA!

Americans will want to disassociate themselves from such types." (p. 23)

Homosexuals know one of the best ways they can implement this propaganda campaign outlined above is through subtle and misleading federal "education" programs in our children's schools. They are also right out there in the open, holding parades, "pride" days, and other festivities to promote the homosexual way of life. Their purpose is clear. As actor Ossie Davis, a homosexual supporter, said, *"You have to fight on every level to achieve the kind of world we'd like to live in."* (Newsday, June 24, 1990)

Another front in the homosexuals' war for legitimacy is the battle to force gays in the military. In 1993, in a blatant attempt to appease homosexual supporters, one of Bill Clinton's first acts as President was to try and force the military to accept open homosexuals in their ranks. On January 29, 1993, Bill Clinton directed Defense Secretary Les Aspin to submit a draft executive order "ending discrimination on the basis of sexual orientation in determining who may serve" in the military in a manner "consistent with the high standards of combat effectiveness and unit cohesion our Armed Forces must maintain."

Radical homosexuals only wanted to lift the ban on gays in the military to try to force middle-America to accept their lifestyle. Lifting the ban on gays in the military was "the No. 1 priority of the homosexual political movement." (USA Today, November 21, 1994) The radical homosexuals and their liberal allies didn't want that truth told because they knew that the vast majority of traditional Americans opposed "normalizing" homosexuality. But as we have clearly demonstrated, the "normalizing" of homosexuality—and the necessary undermining of Christian America—is exactly what these radical secular humanists want.

Crimes Against Children

An under-reported story in the media is that of homosexual child predators. Homosexuals—who make up only 1 or 2% of the entire U.S. population—are responsible for as many as 40% of the child molestation cases in America. The evidence is overwhelming:

• Rev. Paul Shanley, a retired Catholic priest was arrested in San Diego on three counts of child rape. Shanley had a history of molesting boys that went back to 1967. He was at the founding meeting of the North American Man-Boy Love Association (NAMBLA) and while in San Diego operated a bed & breakfast for homosexuals in Palm Springs. Shanley has openly called for "man-boy" love.

• David Carlton Nurmi, was arrested in Florida for possession of child pornography and for molesting a 15-year-old boy.

• Geoffrey Cornish, a well-respected Solana Beach, California therapist was sentenced to 23 years in prison for sexually molesting boys who came to him for therapy. Cornish, who is HIV-positive, was also a coach for the Torrey Pines High School surf team. Cornish told police he had been molested himself by a Boy Scout leader for three years when he was living in England.

• James Edward Sanders, a homosexual child molester, was arrested in New Mexico for sexually abusing a 7-year-old boy. Police also discovered child pornography in Sanders' home.

• Christopher Reardon, a homosexual, former youth minister, and Boy Scout leader was sentenced to 40-50 years in prison for raping, molesting, and disseminating pornography to 29 boys under his care.

Despite the overwhelming evidence, homosexual activists routinely claim that most child molesters are "heterosexual" males, thus trying to shift the focus away from their own very high rates of molestation. Since 98-99% of the population is heterosexual, it is technically correct to say that most molesters are heterosexuals. However, statistics indicate that

WAKE UP, AMERICA!

homosexuals pose a far more serious threat to children than do heterosexuals. For example, Dr. Stephen Rubin of Whitman College conducted a ten-state study of sex abuse cases involving school teachers. Of the 199 cases he studied, 122 male teachers had molested girls, while 14 female teachers had molested boys. He also discovered that 59 homosexual male teachers had molested boys and four female homosexual teachers had molested girls. In other words, 32 percent of those child molestation cases involved homosexuals. Nearly a third of these cases come from only 1-2% of the population.

This high rate of molestations by homosexuals is consistent with other studies conducted during the past several decades. Here are just a few studies that show homosexuals molesting children at epidemic rates:

• The Los Angeles Times conducted a survey of 2,628 adults across the U.S. Of those, 27% of the women and 16% of the men had been sexually molested. Seven percent of the girls and 93% of the men had been molested by adults of the same sex. This means that 40% of child molestations were by homosexuals.

• A Vermont survey of 161 adolescents who were sex offenders found that 35 of them were homosexuals (22%).

• Of the 100 child molesters at the Massachusetts Treatment Center for Sexually Dangerous Persons, a third were heterosexual, a third were bisexual, and a third were homosexual.

• Drs. Freund and Heasman of the Clark Institute of Psychiatry in Toronto reviewed two studies on child molesters and calculated that 34% and 32% of the sex offenders were homosexual. In cases these doctors had handled, 36% of the molesters were homosexuals.

From these studies and many more, it is evident that homosexuals molest children at a far greater rate than do their heterosexual counterparts. While they comprise only 1-2% of the population, they are responsible for upwards of a third or more of all sexual molestations of children.

Homosexuals seldom openly admit that they want to sexually assault children, but their literature and their actions tell another story. In the January 1-8, 2001 issue of *The Weekly Standard*, author Mary Eberstadt exposed the clear link between homosexual activism and the growing North American Man-Boy Love Association (NAMBLA) movement. Writing in, *Pedophilia Chic Reconsidered*: *"The taboo against sex with children continues to erode."*

Eberstadt notes:

The reason why the public is being urged to reconsider boy pedophilia is that this 'question,' settled though it may be in the opinions and laws of the rest of the country, is demonstrably not yet settled within certain parts of the gay rights movement. The more that movement has entered the mainstream, the more this 'question' has bubbled forth from that previously distant realm in the public square.

The homosexual magazine Guide published a pro-pedophile editorial in its July, 1995 issue. In referring to pedophiles as "prophets" of sexual freedom, the Guide editorialist wrote, *"We must listen to our prophets. Instead of fearing being labeled pedophiles, we must proudly proclaim that sex is good, including children's sexuality... Surrounded by pious moralists with deadening anti-sexual rules, we must be shameless rule-breakers, demonstrating our allegiance to a higher concept of love. We must do it for the children's sake."*

Section IV: What are the Effects?

The effects of the war against capitalism, liberty and Christianity in America the past forty-plus years have been both measurable and devastating. Our economy struggles with excessive taxes and heavy government regulations. Our freedoms continue to be chipped away day after day. And our Christian heritage has been beaten nearly into submission.

The outcome of this decline in traditional America has manifested itself in many ways. For example, with the assault on traditional values and the rule of law, Americans no longer seem to have the will to enforce our immigration laws. A flood of illegal immigrants and the balkanization of our nation has been the result. Traditional families in America are being undermined by homosexual activists and other secular humanists. Teenagers in America are in a greater state of crisis than ever before in the history of our nation. And our military forces are left unsupported by half of the nation.

America finds itself in a situation unimaginable by the generation that fought World War II. Can you imagine Americans of that time leaving our borders open at a time of war? Well, the United States is doing just that today. Or how about that generation allowing homosexuals and other secularists to destroy families and put their children in crisis? The people of the United States are doing just that today as well. And can you ever imagine the American people not supporting the troops 100% as they fought the Fascists? Today, our troops are just as likely to be criticized by those secular humanists as they are to be supported by Americans like us.

Sadly, there are many, many more manifestations of the effects of the war against traditional America by these secular humanists. But the effects of illegal immigration, families destroyed, and the balkanization of America alone should be enough to make Americans wake up and take notice.

Section IV: What are the Effects?

Illegal Immigration

★ ★ ★

One of the greatest dangers resulting from the disintegration of America's institutions is the flood of illegal immigrants coming into America. This is a direct threat to both America's security and homogeny. America's security is threatened by the potential for terrorist infiltrators coming in amongst the flood of illegal aliens that cross our border every year. And America's homogeny is threatened by the fact that millions of people with little or no stake in our country or loyalty to our system of government now live in our borders. What reason do these people have to love and protect the things that make America great? What reason do these people have to fight for America when she is threatened? Sadly, very little to none.

And the results are there for all to see. There have been newspaper reports about crowds of fans in Los Angeles cheering Mexico's soccer team over the U.S. team.

Illegal Immigration, Crime and Health

The flood of illegal immigrants into America has contributed to both the skyrocketing rate of violent crime in our country (see Figure 3) and the rise in serious diseases not seen in the United States for years. The facts in this matter are clear:

• **95%** of all outstanding warrants for homicide in Los Angeles are for illegal aliens.

• **94%** of illegal aliens in New York City who come from terrorist nations have disappeared before being deported.

• **One-third** of all the federal prisoners in the U.S. are illegal immigrants.

ILLEGAL IMMIGRATION

- Illegal immigrants in these federal prisons cost taxpayers like you and me over **$1.5 billion** each year.

- An illegal immigrant drug smuggler **murdered a park ranger** in Arizona.

- The vicious illegal immigrant MS-13 gang from El Salvador now operates in **28** American cities.

- **57,600** cars were stolen in Phoenix, Arizona alone by illegal immigrants.

- The Justice Department estimates that illegal immigrant criminals commit an average of **13** crimes each.

- U.S. intelligence says that terrorist organizations have used the lax U.S.-Mexico border to **smuggle terrorist sleeper agents** into this country for the purpose of killing Americans.

- Illegal aliens are responsible for the **14,871** new cases of tuberculosis that have popped up in Michigan, Florida, Virginia, Georgia, Colorado, Texas and dozens of other states.

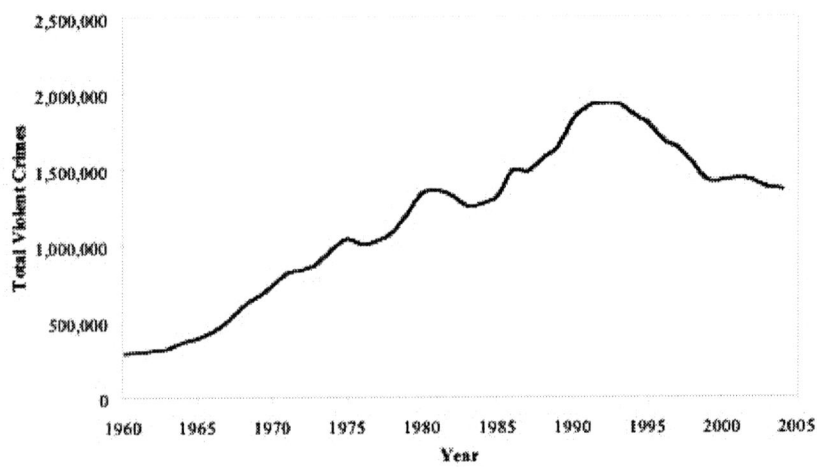

Figure 3. Violent Crimes Rate.
Source: Disaster Center Website; U.S. Dept Justice, Bureau of Justice Statistics

WAKE UP, AMERICA!

Rampant crime. A drastically increased terrorist threat. More and more tax dollars being spent on federal prisons. And now brand new outbreaks of diseases like tuberculosis, which was once completely wiped out of America. ALL are the result of the massive wave of illegal immigrants that have flooded our country. And this threat reaches all the way to our nation's capital: In the suburbs of Washington, D.C., the MS-13 gang of El Salvadorian illegal immigrants are using machetes to cut the hands off people who wander into their "turf".

How can illegal immigrants be responsible for so much of the crime in America? Often, the cities where illegal immigrant crime is highest, the police are actually forbidden from arresting them for being illegal in the first place! In Los Angeles, for example, members of a ruthless Salvadoran prison gang run rampant in the city. Their status as illegal immigrants is a felony. Yet the police are forbidden from arresting these violent gang members because it's against the rules in Los Angeles to enforce America's immigration laws. This rule against enforcing America's immigration laws can also be found in New York, Chicago, San Diego, Austin, and Houston, to name a few places.

Rules like this prove beyond a doubt the power of the anti-American, secular-socialist forces that have taken control of so many aspects of American life. Traditional Americans would never (and still do not!) tolerate such protections for foreigners who broke our laws and came to our country illegally. But the secular-socialists in America see these illegal immigrants as a source of power for them. Millions of people living in the United States owe their very lives in the country to these forces protecting them. And these illegal immigrants often do whatever the secular-socialists ask of them. This dangerous alliance, if allowed to continue unopposed, will threaten the very fabric of our nation.

National Security Problems

The millions of illegal immigrants flooding the United States endanger

Illegal Immigration

the national security of America. First and foremost, any of these millions of illegal immigrants we allow to pour over our border unchecked could be Al Qaeda terrorists bent on wreaking destruction in America. It is true that most of the 9/11 terrorists were in the United States illegally, and yet nothing was done about it. More Muslim illegal immigrants are crossing into our country every day, creating a severe U.S. security threat. Despite recent enforcement reforms and crackdowns by the United States and by Mexican President Vincente Fox, illegal immigration continues steadily. Only a comprehensive effort to stop the trafficking of illegal immigrants over our border, combined with the rounding up of every illegal immigrant already in the United States, will be sure to prevent another 9/11 terrorist attack on our country by illegal foreigners.

Economic Costs

The economic price of illegal immigration to American taxpayers is massive. Illegal immigrants already receive:

- Welfare benefits, including food stamps.
- Free health care.
- Free hospitalization for childbirth.
- Free schooling in *Spanish*.

Most Americans don't get these taxpayer-funded handouts. Why in the world should *Mexicans who came to America illegally?* And if the millions of illegal immigrants who are in the country right now stay throughout their lifetimes, the Washington Times reports taxpayers would be soaked to the tune of $30 billion a year to support them. This is an outrageous abuse of the American taxpayer and must be rectified immediately.

FAMILIES DESTROYED
★ ★ ★

The erosion of marriage and the destruction of the traditional family during the past forty-plus years have resulted in large-scale negative effects on both children and adults. In fact, it lies at the heart of many of the social problems in America today. Children raised without a father in the home are more likely to experience emotional and behavioral problems, school failure, drug and alcohol abuse, crime, and incarceration. The beneficial effects of marriage on individuals and society are beyond reasonable dispute. And yet, after years of assault by secular humanists, the decline of traditional marriage continues unabated.

Some argue that we should not "interfere" in the private decisions concerning marriage of others. This is a bad argument because the decline of marriage affects us all. When the crime rate goes up, it is the American people who are the victims. Taxpayers are forced to subsidize single parent families to the tune of $150 billion each year. In truth, the growth of single-parent families has had an enormous impact on the growth of government. Much of this taxpayer funded expenditure could be avoided if the mothers were married to the fathers of their children. Liberals insist that we taxpayers have an obligation to support single parents and to mitigate the damage that results from the erosion of marriage. But instead, shouldn't we fight to reverse the decline of marriage in the first place?

Nearly one-third of all American children are born outside marriage (Figure 4). That's one out-of-wedlock birth every 35 seconds in America. And over the past forty-plus years, the increase in illegitimacy has grown alarmingly.

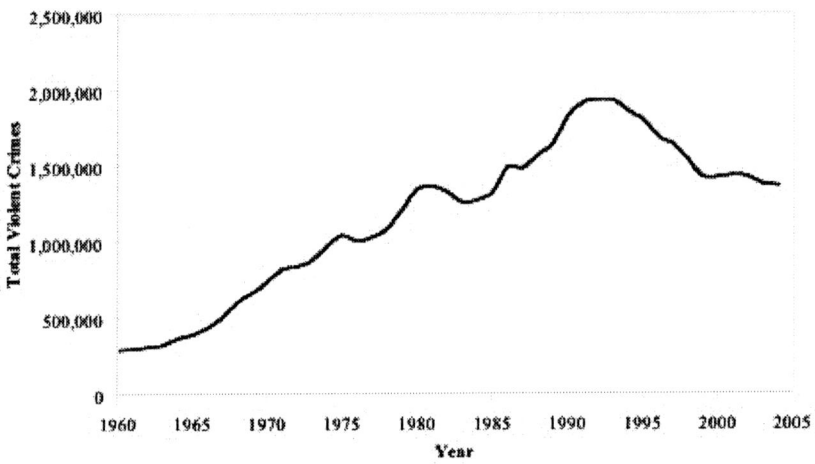

Figure 3. Violent Crimes Rate.
Source: Disaster Center Website; U.S. Dept Justice, Bureau of Justice Statistics

Of those born inside marriage, a great many children will experience their parents' divorce before they reach age 18. More than half of the children in the United States will spend all or part of their childhood in never-formed or broken families. And even though the divorce rate in America has declined some recently (thank God), as you can see in Figure 5 and the statistics just cited, the rate of divorce in America is still far too high.

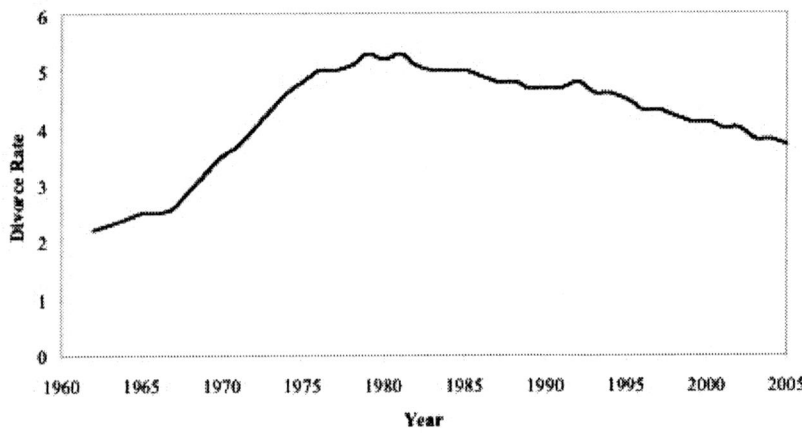

Figure 5. American Divorce Rate (per 1000 people).
Source: United States Census Bureau, National Center for Health Statistics

Wake Up, America!

The collapse of marriage is the principal cause of child poverty in the United States. Children raised by never-married mothers are seven times more likely to live in poverty than children raised by their biological parents in intact marriages. Overall, approximately 80 percent of long-term child poverty in the United States occurs among children from broken or never-formed families.

One expert, David Popenoe, in his testimony before the Committee on Ways and Means in the United States House of Representatives, put the damage of broken homes to children in these stark terms:

"Much of the linkage between the decline of marriage and the rise of problems in childhood rests with the absent father. The evidence is now strong that fathers do matter in the lives of their children. And, although there are many caring and responsible non-resident fathers, the alarmingly simple fact is that men are much less likely to stay close to their children when they are not married to their children's mother. Men tend to view marriage and childrearing as a single package. If they are not married or are divorced, their interest in and sense of responsibility toward children greatly diminish. Many studies have found that a high percentage of all unmarried or divorced fathers lose regular contact with their children over time."

Why is marriage so important to fatherhood? Because being a father is universally problematic for men in a way it is not for women. Put simply, as marriage weakens, fathers stray. While mothers the world over bear and nurture their young with an intrinsic acknowledgement of their role, fathers are often filled with conflict and doubt. Left culturally unregulated, men's sexual behavior can be promiscuous, their paternity casual, their commitment to families weak. Marriage is society's way of engaging the basic problem of fatherhood — how to hold the father to the stronger mother-child bond. As a cultural institution, marriage stresses the long-run commitment of the male, the durability of the marital relationship, and the importance of the union for children.

Our national goal should be no less than to rebuild a marriage culture, one in which as many children as possible grow up with their fathers and mothers providing care and nurture and stability. We should be every bit as much concerned with our nation's family environment as we are with our nation's economic and natural environments. Yet if ever there was a serious domestic problem almost entirely ignored by our national elected representatives, this is it. Despite the fact, for example, that many Americans believe the current state of marriage to be one of the major problems of our time, no high-level government body in memory has examined the issue. Indeed, in recent years the government even has cut back on the collection of marriage statistics.

Is the goal of renewing a marriage-based society impossible to achieve? It certainly will not be easy. Much of the needed change must come, of course, in the cultural, moral and spiritual realms. But there are many things that can be done at the federal level to smooth the path. Perhaps the most important is merely to recognize—as societies in the past have nearly always done as a part of public policy—that the benefits to children of having married parents are so great that the institution of marriage should be encouraged by every reasonable means possible. Fortunately, many ways exist to strengthen and stabilize marriage, to make marriage a more satisfying as well as more durable social relationship. And, of course, government should seek to do no harm in this realm. It should never institute policies, for example, that provide disincentives to marriage, or that fail equally to support children not in a two-parent family.

Some believe that pro-marriage policies can not be put forth without stigmatizing and penalizing those who for one reason or another, sometimes through no fault of their own, are not married. Yet the fact remains that the overwhelming majority of young people today wish to marry for life, and the parents of these young people, no matter what their marital state, also hold that goal for their offspring. There is actually an enormous reservoir of support for a marriage-based culture. In addition to the significant and enduring benefits for children, the evidence is clear that having a solid, long-term marriage greatly enhances the wealth, health, longevity, and overall happiness of adults.

More than 2000 years ago the Roman statesman Cicero noted that "marriage is the first bond of society." Surely this observation is no less true today."

WAKE UP, AMERICA!

Homosexual Attacks on Marriage

Traditional marriage—the union between one man and one woman—has been the norm in all of human history. It is the basic unit of society, and it is the place where character, love, empathy, skills, and morality are taught. As social researcher Amitai Etzioni has written,

"There never was a society throughout all of history...without a family as the central unit for launching the education of children, for character formation, and as the moral agent of society."

The family has universally been understood to be a joining of a man and a woman in marriage for the purpose of building a life together and having children. In order to develop properly, children need to be living in a stable home with a mother and father. Boys and girls need both a mom and dad in order to learn what it means to be male and female. When one of these parents is missing from the family unit, it can cause great devastation to children. David Blankenhorn, writing in Fatherless America: Confronting Our Most Urgent Social Problem, observes, *"Fatherlessness—the absence of paternal transmission—contributes to a decline of character and competence in children."* For boys, this frequently translates into drug abuse and criminal behavior; for girls, it typically means sexual promiscuity, abortion, and welfare. Mothers are equally important in the development of a child's character. Dr. Brenda Hunter, a Christian psychologist, has written extensively on the importance of motherhood. In her book, *The Power of Mother Love*, she writes to moms:

"Without our presence, our love, our empathy, many of our children will grow up emotionally handicapped, unable to say a timely word to a hurting friend or to reach out to the less fortunate. Others—and their number are increasing—may even become brutal, remorseless killers."

Homosexual activists, however, are determined to overturn the natural order of things by subverting and redefining marriage. Homosexual activist Michelangelo Signorile, writing in Out magazine, makes this clear. He says homosexuals should fight for same-sex marriage and its benefits and then, once granted, redefine the institution of marriage completely...to debunk a myth and radically alter an archaic institution...The most subversive action lesbians and gays can undertake—and one that would perhaps benefit all of society—is to transform the notion of 'family' entirely.

Homosexuals won a significant victory against the God-ordained institution of marriage when the Vermont Supreme Court ordered the state legislature to grant homosexuals the same rights and benefits as given to traditional marriages. The Court issued its decision in response to a lawsuit brought by several homosexual "lovers" who claimed they were being denied the right to marry. The Vermont legislature subsequently passed a "civil union" law. This civil union law confers the same basic benefits upon homosexual couples as it does for husband and wife marriages. This includes the right to inherit property; to make life and death medical decisions; to share medical and insurance policies; and to file joint tax returns. The civil union law, however, is different than traditional marriage. And legalization of gay marriage was the next victory for the homosexual activists, this time in Massachusetts. A razor-thin state Supreme Court majority overturned the clearly expressed will of the people (even in ultra-liberal Massachusetts) and forced the state to recognize homosexual marriage. Now the door is open for homosexual marriages in all 49 other states in the country.

By why are homosexual radicals so bent on legalizing gay marriage anyway? Homosexuals are notoriously promiscuous. Even if allowed to marry, they will continue to seek multiple partnerships. Homosexual Andrew Sullivan is the senior editor at *The New Republic*. In his book, *Virtually Normal*, he says that straight society will learn a lot from homosexual marriages if they are legalized. He notes that straights will learn to have a greater, *"understanding of the need for extramarital outlets between two men than between a man and a woman."* In other words, homosexuals have no intention of remaining monogamous to each other, as you should expect in a marriage. Sullivan criticizes what he calls the "stifling model of heterosexual normality." In short, homosexuals are seeking to destroy traditional marriage to normalize same-sex marriages (including multiple sex partners). If homosexual marriages are legalized, polygamy will not be far behind. And this can only serve to erode the institution of traditional marriage even further.

The Battle for the Unborn

Another major cause of the decline of families is the legalization of abortion. The battle over abortion is perhaps the most important and most divisive ethical issue in America. Ever since the 1973 *Roe v. Wade* Supreme Court decision allowing abortion to become legal, liberal courts have continued to sacrifice the lives of millions of unborn children at the altar of radical feminism. In the name of "privacy," doctors are permitted under the law to abort babies still in their mother's womb. And in the guise of foreign aid, American taxpayers have been asked to fund the export of this terrible destruction of the unborn to the entire world.

Following the 1973 *Roe v. Wade* Supreme Court decision making abortion legal, radical abortion proponents launched a massive campaign to institutionalize abortion in American life. And the key to institutionalizing abortion was to require that federal funds be made available to women to have their abortions subsidized by the taxpayers. By 1977, Medicaid (and thus the taxpayers) were helping to fund 300,000 abortions each year, at the cost of $50 million. (Washington Post, June 30, 1977) Senator Jesse Helms at the time called abortion, *"deliberate termination of an innocent human life"* and lamented that *"a requirement that taxpayers furnish the money to terminate innocent human life...killing a group of human beings...I don't think she [a pregnant woman] should have the right to use tax funds to terminate another life for her convenience."* (Washington Post, June 30, 1977)

FAMILIES DESTROYED

Without a doubt, the scourge of legalized abortion in America is one of the greatest shames in our nation's history. As bad as slavery was in the United States, did it kill more innocent Americans that the 40 million that abortion has? Six million Jews died in the Holocaust. But that pales in comparison to the number of innocent babies that have been murdered by abortionists. Until Americans wake up and right this incredible wrong, I fear that our nation will never be right with God.

Children in Crisis

The most common victims of the secular war against traditional families in America are, as you might imagine, the children. The fundamental function of families as an institution is to protect, nurture and raise children. But with the dissolution of traditional families, the difficulties the nation's children face have grown precipitously. In addition to the dangers to children posed by the dissolution of traditional families, our children are also being very poorly served by the secular-socialist assaults against education in America. A combination of the crumbling of the institution of the family with the rapid deterioration of traditional education have put our nation's children in a state of nearly perpetual crisis.

Education

Liberal bureaucrats have taken almost complete control of public education in America. These "educrats" have downplayed most vestiges of traditional education—reading, writing and arithmetic—and turned public education into a giant secular-socialist Petri dish. Instead of educating children, they make claims about "preparing them for life" and other nonsense. The results are so ridiculous that they would be laughable were they not so sad. A child in public schools today needs written parental permission to get an aspirin from the school nurse, but a school guidance counselor can assist a 13 year old with getting an abortion without the parents ever even being informed. And high school seniors are graduating well versed in the use of condoms, but unable to read at even a basic level.

This tragic state of affairs is even more infuriating when you consider the massive amount of taxpayer money pouring down the public education rat hole. Figure 6 shows K-12 education spending from 1965 through today. The amount of taxpayer money spend on public education has skyrocketed over the past 40 years. But that contrasts greatly with the Scholastic Aptitude Test (SAT) results shown in Figure 7. Test results for public school students are much lower than they were in 1965, despite all of the hundreds of millions of dollars spent on public education! Clearly, the American taxpayers are not getting virtually any return on our investment in education. The blame lies squarely at the feet of the public education bureaucrats, who've concentrated more on banning prayer and the Ten Commandments and promoting condoms than actually teaching math and history and science.

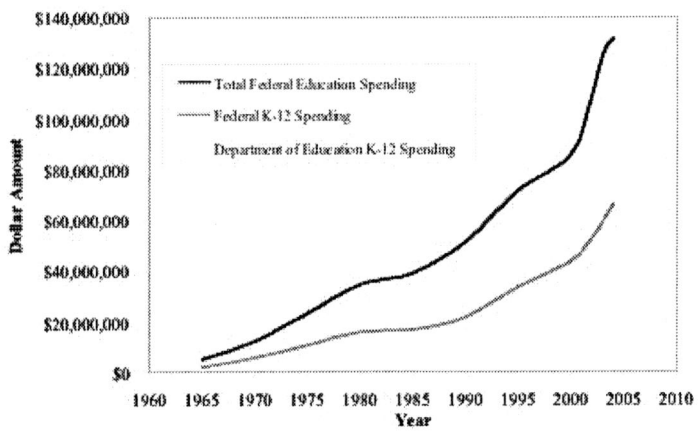

Figure 6. Total Federal Spending on K-12 Education.
Source: U.S. Department of Education, National Center for Education Statistics

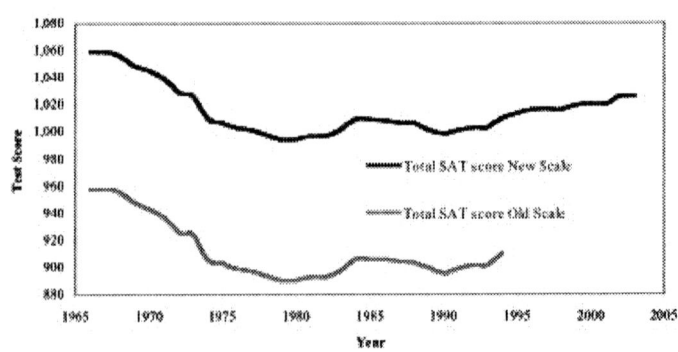

Figure 7. Scholastic Aptitude Test (SAT) Scores.
Source: U.S. Department of Education, National Center for Education Statistics,

WAKE UP, AMERICA!

Sex Education

Sadly, the one type of education that public schools seem proficient with these days is that of sex. Our children are already inundated with sex in today's culture, from commercials to MTV to magazines and billboards. Sex is everywhere. And naturally, children are curious. But this is a matter for the parents to intervene, not the schools. Parents have the right to educate their children about sex the way they want—especially in concordance with their religious values. Public schools have banned virtually all aspects of religion. But religion and morality are the basis upon which children are taught about abstinence and responsibility in regards to sex. Without religion in public schools, all that is left is a tacit acceptance that teenagers are free to have as much sex as they want with as many partners as they care to—without moral, psychological or physical consequences. That is why the primary aspect of sex education in public schools is how to practice "safe" sex. But the only safe sex for unmarried teenagers is abstinence. It protects from both disease and unwanted pregnancy (and by extension the holocaust of abortion) every time. On the other hand, the consequences of "safe" sex education in public schools have been devastating to children. Sexual diseases are rampantly growing in our population (see Figure 8 on growth of the Sexually Transmitted Disease (STD) Chlamydia, for example), in large part due to the huge jump in the rate of teen sexual activity. This huge jump in teen STDs occurred as a direct result of the "safe" sex teachings in public schools that really did nothing more than promote promiscuity amongst our nation's children.

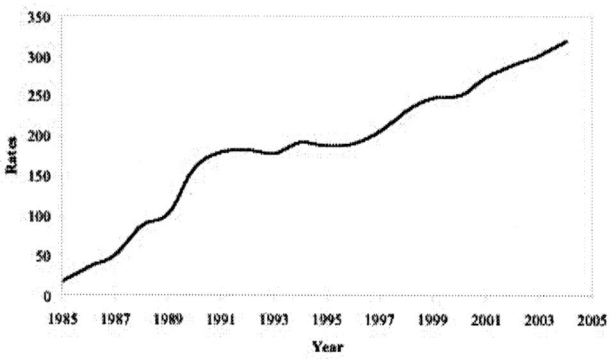

Figure 8. Chlamydia Rates (per 100,000 civilian population).
Source: Department of Health and Human Services, Centers for Disease Control and Prevention

Children in Crisis

Drug Use

Drug use among teenagers is a terrible problem in America. Figure 9 shows the alarmingly high and alarmingly steady rate of drug use among American 12th graders. The dissolution of the family and the takeover of public education by liberal bureaucrats have contributed to the massive rate of drug use among teenagers. But these are not the single greatest causes of the huge rise in teen drug use. The facts show that drug use among teens grew rapidly at the same time that the moral guidance provided by God and prayer was stamped out of our children's public schools.

Our Founding Fathers would be horrified if, during their tenure, illegal drugs replaced prayer in school. Yet today, more and more children are bringing drugs to school and even using them during class. And at the same time, these children are being forced to leave their faith at home—because God is an outlaw in America's schools.

Ever since a liberal Supreme Court first banned school prayer in the early 1960s, our country has been morally decaying—that is an undeniable fact. It's a fact—our schools have churned out more murderers, more rapists, and more robbers than ever before. It's a fact—we see more schoolgirls getting pregnant and either having abortions or giving birth to babies without a father in the home—babies on welfare. And it is a very sad fact—we've had more schoolchildren turn to drugs to escape the realities of life—who find inspiration in crack-cocaine instead of their faith.

Each generation has strayed farther away from the basic values that our parents and grandparents instilled in us as they've gotten farther away from prayer in school. And the massive and sustained rates of teen drug abuse seen in Figure 9 is clearly the tragic result.

WAKE UP, AMERICA!

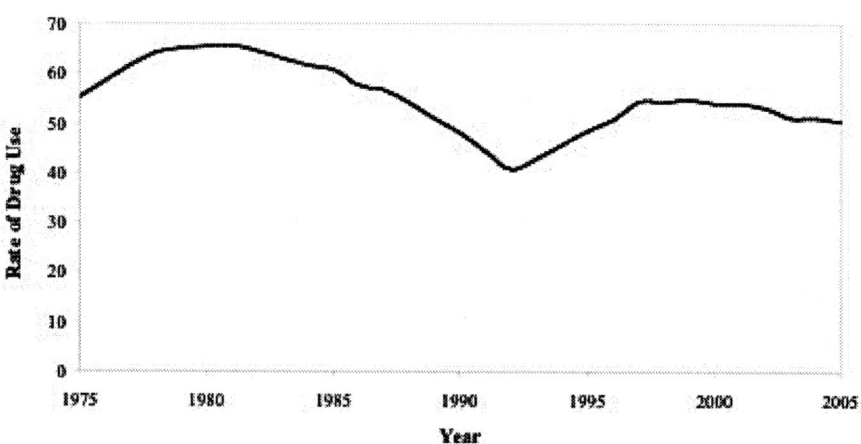

Figure 9. Drug Use Among 12th Graders.
Source: www.monitoringthefuture.org

Undermining Our Military and War Effort

★ ★ ★

Secular-socialist liberals in America don't support our troops and undermine America's war effort against Islamic terrorists. Yes, this is a bold statement. But it has the virtue of being true. Historically, liberals have opposed nearly every defense spending and military program proposed in Congress. Not only do our troops suffer the consequences of this lack of supplies and modern weaponry, our troops also suffer serious morale problems knowing that parts of the country don't even appreciate what they sacrifice for the rest of us. And because our troops are not fully armed, with their morale in doubt, our nation's ability to fight wars is seriously undermined. No matter how much liberals may protest to the contrary, the fact of the matter is you can never legitimately say you support the troops but don't support the war. By failing to support the war, liberals undercut the troops fighting this war and undermine our nation's war effort.

This undermining of America's war effort is not a new one to the forces of secular-socialism. For most of the 50-year era, liberals opposed the Cold War against Soviets. Many liberals actually spied against our own country for the Soviets (for example, State Department official Alger Hiss). Others opposed every proposal that would help America win the Cold War—from a missile defense system to Ronald Reagan's military buildup.

Liberals were wrong then, and they are wrong today in the War on Terror. The ACLU, elite media and other liberals are doing all they can to undermine our war effort today. Here's just one glaring example: On Dec. 16, 2005 the *New York Times* ran a front page news story exposing America's secret program to eavesdrop on Al Qaeda terrorists:

Months after the Sept. 11 attacks, President Bush secretly authorized the

Undermining Our Military and War Effort

National Security Agency (NSA) to eavesdrop on Americans and others inside the United States to search for evidence of terrorist activities....

It is bad enough the New York Times made it seem like President Bush was eavesdropping on innocent Americans, which he was not. The only Americans that were being spied on were those who were talking to Al Qaeda terrorists. But worse than that was the fact that the New York Times revealed America's top secret spy program to our enemies on the front page of their paper! Just days after this article came out, suspected terrorists within the United States were found to have bought large numbers of untraceable disposable cell phones at numerous stores around the country, according to ABC news. This was clearly in response to the leak by the NYT that told our terrorist enemies our government was trying to eavesdrop on their conversations. President Bush said the New York Times story, *"damages our national security and puts our citizens at risk"* and called the decision to publish this top-secret information a *"shameful act."* CIA director Porter Goss told Congress that, *"the damage has been very severe to our capabilities to carry out our mission...I use the words 'very severe' intentionally."* And Attorney General Alberto Gonzales lamented, *"I cannot help but wonder if [our enemies] aren't shaking their heads in amazement at the thought that anyone would imperil such a sensitive program by leaking its existence in the first place, and smiling at the prospect that we might have to disclose even more or perhaps even unilaterally disarm ourselves of a key tool in the war on terror."*

If an American newspaper revealed the same kind of secret to the Nazis during World War II, the reporters would have been charged with treason. But today, this undermining of our war effort continues by anti-American forces at the New York Times and other liberal newspapers, at American universities, at the ACLU and other such groups, and even at the highest levels of the Democratic party.

Military Shows Signs of Wear

Today, America's military forces are still trying to recover from 8 years of draconian military budget cuts during the Clinton Administration. Figure 10 shows the number of American military forces in the 1990s. See for yourself how drastic the drop was.

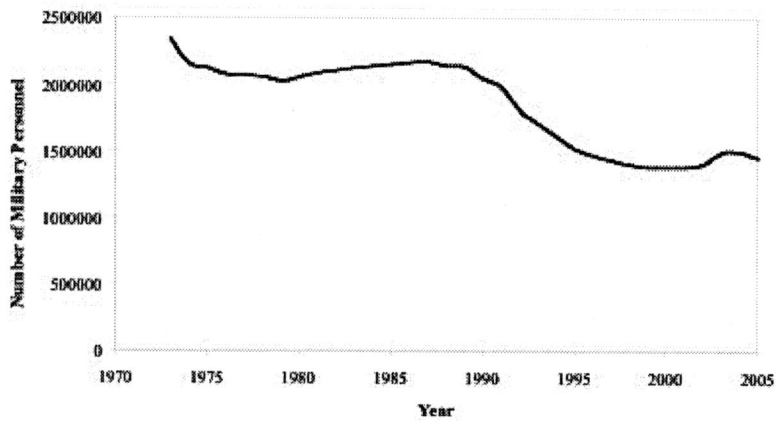

Figure 10. U.S. Military Force Levels.
Source: www.defenselink.mil

After the 9/11 attacks on America, our government reversed this disastrous trend and began to increase both funding and the size of our military forces. But even today, as you can see on the military forces graph, the strength of America's military is still far below where it was in the first Persian Gulf War just 16 years ago. And this is all a result of average Americans and our elected officials sitting back and allowing the liberal secular-socialists to wage an eight year scorched earth assault on the U.S. military in the 1990s.

The American people and our elected officials need to make a concerted effort to restore U.S. military forces to full strength as soon as possible. Especially today, when our troops are fighting and dying in what will be a very long war against Islamic terrorists, we should do no less. If Americans fail in this task to fully support and fully fund our military forces, we will surely lose the war with Islamic terrorists. And for our catastrophic failure to support the troops, we will have deserved this terrible fate.

Balkanization of America

★ ★ ★

America used to be a united nation. The words on our currency, *e pluribus unum*, are Latin for *"from many, one."* It conveys the idea that the many immigrants who come from so many different nations all enter our great melting pot and become Americans, embracing our culture, language and ideals. But today, the opposite is often true. Instead of encouraging immigrants to learn English and become Americans, liberal activists are helping foreigners keep their own language and culture while living in America. This is a terribly dangerous trend, one that in the future could rip America apart. Just look at the problems Canada faces today. The French and English speaking citizens of Canada have never really learned to live together in one nation, and have often come close to splitting Canada apart. The same fate could be in store for America. The United States being overrun by illegal immigrants, most of which are not assimilating to our culture. At soccer events in Los Angeles, as mentioned earlier, the crowds very often cheer for the Mexican team over the United States. This in and of itself is not a catastrophe. But it is symptomatic of a much larger problem. If these immigrants will cheer for their homeland's team over the U.S. team, even if they live in America now, they will also remain loyal to their homeland at the expense of America's security and homogeny. For all intents and purposes, America is allowing a potentially hostile fifth column to germinate within our borders.

Another dire threat to American unity comes from the issue of granting Puerto Rico statehood. The political status of Puerto Rico has always been a controversial issue ever since the island nation was ceded by Spain after the U.S. victory in the Spanish-American War in 1898. U.S. citizenship was granted in 1917 giving Puerto Rico "Commonwealth" status with all the rights of Americans except voting in presidential elections and having voting representation in Congress, rights accorded only to states.

BALKANIZATION OF AMERICA

Former Puerto Rican governor Carlos Romero-Barcelo makes it perfectly clear why Puerto Ricans want statehood:

The State of Puerto Rico will qualify for a great deal of federal aid money ...Puerto Rico's per capita contribution to the federal treasury, were we a state, would come to less than that of any other state in the Union. At the same time the per capita benefits we'd reap from federal aid programs would be the greater than those of any other state in the Union. On top of all this we'd also have seven or eight Puerto Ricans serving as full voting members of Congress, working up in Washington at all times to help draft and pass new and improved social welfare legislation.

Puerto Rico is a desperately impoverished island where 60% of its 3.7 million inhabitants subsist on U.S. Food Stamps. That is a rate more than twice as high than that of Mississippi, the poorest U.S. state. Statehood would eliminate current caps on welfare and make the island eligible for some $3 billion in additional public assistance. A study conducted by Peat Marwick states that Puerto Rican statehood would inevitably result in a net annual revenue deficit for the Federal Government totaling $25 billion! The study concludes that statehood would result in a permanent drop of 10-15% in Puerto Rican national products with an accompanying loss of up to 145,000 jobs, furthering a hopeless dependency on the already strained American taxpayer. Consider these basic facts:

• Puerto Rico suffers from an unemployment rate of about 20%.

• Two-thirds of the Puerto Rican population live below the federal poverty level.

• An unbelievable 60% of Puerto Rican children born on the U.S. mainland are born to unwed mothers (more than twice the national average and far greater than any other Hispanic group in the U.S.)

WAKE UP, AMERICA!

- Our own government has projected that as a state Puerto Rico would get as much as $4 billion in assistance from the American taxpayers annually.

- As a state, Puerto Rican residents would start getting about $400 a month in federal welfare payments.

- Less than 20% of Puerto Ricans speak English. Only 16% consider themselves to be American. And according to *The New York Times*, "Fully 90 percent of the island's public school students lack basic English skills by the time they graduate."

The problem of speaking English is the most volatile issue to the Puerto Ricans. The island has a history of pride in their culture and language and has always fought with great resistance all measures to extend English in their schools. As reported in the *New York Post* the liberal opponents to English, *"might well become a powerful institutional voice for making Spanish a quasi-official language of the U.S."* The residents of Puerto Rico, even though they receive large federal education funding grants, do not have access to a public English language education. If Puerto Rico became a state, we would create a Quebec-like enclave of linguistic separatism in Puerto Rico. And don't think for one minute that Puerto Ricans would learn English if they became a state. Carlos Romero-Barcelo remains firm in opposition to English: *"Yes, we want statehood, but...neither our language nor our culture is negotiable."*

Homegrown Terrorism

America has its hands full fighting Muslim terrorists. But Puerto Rican statehood would lead directly to a whole new batch of terrorists with which to contend—that of Puerto Rican separatists. The media doesn't cover this issue much, but Puerto Rican terrorists have been attacking America for decades.

BALKANIZATION OF AMERICA

There are various terrorist groups emanating in Puerto Rico that have infiltrated the U.S. in the past several years. The most deadly groups include the following:

- Fuerzas Amadas de Liberacion Nacional (FALN) - responsible for more than 130 bombings since the mid 1970s.
- Comandos Amados de Liberacion (CAL)
- Movimiento Independista Revolucionario Armada (MIR)
- Fuerzas Armadas de Resistencia Popular (FARP)
- Comandos Revolucionarios del Pueblo (CRP)
- Los Macheteros (literally the "machete wielders")

These groups have been responsible for attacks on military installations (including the destruction of several National Guard fighter jets worth over $50 million), federal buildings (including a rocket attack on the FBI offices in San Juan) and armed robbery of over $7 million to finance their terrorist operations throughout the U.S. Carlos Ayes, a terrorist suspect, was quoted by The *New York Times Magazine* stating, "*Statehood will mean war. If the United States wants its very own Northern Ireland, let them continue this farce.*" For those who take this as just an idle threat, remember the anti-American Puerto Rican terrorists who once tried to assassinate President Truman and shot up the House of Representatives in 1954.

Presently there is a small but militant faction that continues to fight for Puerto Rican independence. You can be sure that this belligerent group would react violently to Puerto Rican statehood. They include among their supporters the most militant band of thugs in the world today; and they continually make threats against the U.S., decrying a century of "Yankee Imperialism."

Should the liberals succeed in their attempt to grant Puerto Rican statehood, it could trigger terrorism by nationalist militants who are determined to maintain independence at any cost. Any attempt to absorb cultural differences could also lead the U.S. down the road of Quebec and Ireland, as mentioned, and other countries that have fought bloody wars when minority populations tried to maintain a separate language and identity within another nation.

The Puerto Ricans want all the welfare and aid they can get from American taxpayers, but in return they have done nothing to protect or assist American citizens from even their own terrorists. Americans must not sit idly by and allow this disastrous statehood scheme to pass. The reason is both clear and urgent: Puerto Rican statehood would contribute to the further erosion of American greatness. Puerto Rico would be a welfare nightmare for American taxpayers. Government programs would continue to grow to support Puerto Rico as a state, and thus contribute to the further erosion of small government and capitalism in our nation. And though Puerto Rico is a Christian culture, it does not have the same traditions as American Christians do in regard to government. The further tearing of our social fabric in this regard would be disastrous.

Section V: The War Outside America

From the end of the Cold War to the September 11, 2001 terrorist attacks, the American people were lulled into a sense of security from the world outside. Americans believed—and this belief was encouraged by an irresponsible Clinton administration and its sycophantic media—that the dangers from evil foreign states were a relic of the past. We had nothing to worry about anymore. Yes, America would on occasion send military forces to deal with ethnic cleansing in Bosnia, for example. But there really was not any great foreign threat to America, at least not on the scale we faced in Nazi Germany and Soviet Russia. Nothing could have been further from the truth.

On September 11th, 2001, our blissful ignorance was shattered by planes crashing into the World Trade Center and the Pentagon. Obviously, the threat of Islamic terrorists, especially in an age of weapons of mass destruction, dominates our national security thoughts today. And for good reason: The Islamic threat to America is a dire one. But too many of our leaders are not taking the Islamic threat seriously enough. Politically correct thinking pervades the liberal elite circles, and they often seem more concerned about protecting the rights of terrorists than protecting Americans from those terrorists. That is the first major threat to our national security.

The second major threat to America's security is related to the first. Weapons of mass destruction in the hands of terrorists are a dire threat to America. But just as dangerous are weapons of mass destruction wielded by Communist China or other rogue states. Right now, America has no defense against a nuclear missile attack launched from China or Iran or anyone else for that matter. This terrible vulnerability is a relic of the Cold War "mutual assured destruction" policy, and it must be rectified immediately to protect the American people. If you thought the damage done by the terrorists on 9/11 was bad, imagine the destruction wrought by a nuclear attack on the major cities of the United States. Our nation would be hard pressed even to survive. This is not a security threat that the media covers much, if at all. But a defense against missile-launched weapons of mass destruction should be a top priority for the United States.

Another seldom covered security threat to America comes from Communist China. The American media often portrays Communist China as an economic rival at worst. But the truth is the Red Chinese are on a strategic level collision course with the United States over domination of the Pacific Rim. The flashpoint of this confrontation is most likely to be America's ally, Taiwan. Red China wants to take over this country, by force if necessary. And they are preparing their military forces to be able to do just that. Moreover, the Red Chinese are preparing their military forces to confront the United States military if and when a conflict results. Even if the Chinese military is defeated in such a conflict, the communist leaders of that country have one more ace up their sleeve—nuclear weapons. Red China has an arsenal of nuclear missiles that can reach the United States, and we can do nothing about it. Does anyone doubt that China's brutal leadership would happily sacrifice millions, even hundreds of millions, of their own people to destroy the United States and emerge as the leading power in the world? A serious policy of standing up to Communist China and containing their expansionist ambitions must be undertaken by the United States. To date, no such policy has been implemented.

Finally, though not a direct military threat, the danger posed by international socialism and the United Nations is no less real to the United States. International socialists seek to undermine our capitalist system, restrict our liberty, and destroy our Christian heritage from without. And the United Nations is often complicit in these endeavors. American policymakers need to stop looking at the United Nations and international socialists as irrelevant factions or even benign forces and begin to deal with them as the threats they truly are.

These external threats are not directly contributing to the decline of the pillars of greatness of the United States. However, the dangers of radical Islam, nuclear missile attack, an aggressive communist regime in China, and international socialism and the United Nations are directly related to the thesis of this book. All of these external forces put more and more pressure on a declining American power base. As the United States continues to fall victim to the forces that are destroying what makes our country great, Americans will have a harder and harder time dealing forcefully with these external threats. And the consequences of this decline in American power can be dire for our nation. Any one of the four external threats described in this section can utterly destroy America. Radical Islam can bring constant terrorism and suicide bombings to our very own home towns. An Iranian or North Korean or Red Chinese nuclear missile attack could destroy every major city in the United States. Red China could spark a war in the Pacific that engulfs the entire Pacific Rim—from Korea to Japan to the U.S. West Coast—in flames. International socialists could destroy the world economic system, plunging the United States into unending depression. And the United Nations, in addition to trying to impinge upon our sovereignty and raid our tax dollars, could also help provide cover for all of these potential threats to prevent the U.S. from taking strong action to protect its citizens.

Section V: The War Outside

Radical Islam

★ ★ ★

The War on Terrorism, whether politicians and pundits want to admit it or not, is in actuality a clash of civilizations between the Islamic world and the Christian world. More specifically, the War on Terrorism boils down to a Holy War declared by Muslims against Christianity in America and Europe. In the Dark Ages, Muslims went to war against Christian Europe, and nearly destroyed it. In the Middle Ages, the Christian kingdoms of Europe counter-attacked the Muslims during the Crusades in an attempt to recapture the Holy Land. After centuries of back-and-forth fighting, the Christian states of Europe eventually conquered and colonized most of the Islamic world. But the Muslim states are the ones on the offensive today. After the rapid decolonization of the Muslim world post-World War II, anti-Christian Islamic radicalism began to re-assert itself. And make no mistake about it. No matter what you hear about Islam being a religion of peace or any other propaganda, the fact is Muslims have declared Jihad—Holy War—against the Christian world.

America is now at war with the Muslim world. This is not a war that America wanted or started, but it is a war that they have declared against us nonetheless. And if the United States does not treat this war against Islam as a real war that must be fought and won, America will lose this war. Just look at Figure 11 to see for yourself how outnumbered the United States is by Muslims in the world, and how many more Muslims there will be by 2025.

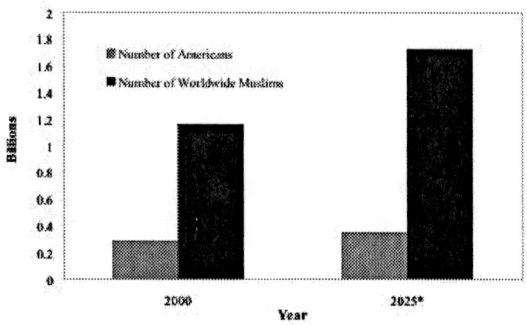

Figure 11. U.S. Population and Worldwide Muslim Population (*Data for 2025 are projected figures).
Source: *United States Census Bureau*

tion numbers. We are also at a disadvantage with our allies. The Muslim radicals are not just at war with America. They are also at war with what they consider to be Christian Europe as well. The problem for America is that most of Europe is no longer really Christian. And since Europeans don't view this clash of civilizations as their fight as well, most of Europe is unwilling to fight this war. America is basically without any allies in this colossal struggle. You don't need to look any further than the train bombing in Madrid, Spain to prove this point. The Spanish were giving the United States support and even troops to help fight the war in Iraq. But Al Qaeda terrorists exploded a bomb on a train in the Spanish capital, Madrid. Rather than wake the Spanish people up to the dire threat the Muslims posed to Europe, this attack prompted the Spanish people to vote out the pro-American government and vote in an anti-American government that pulled out all of their troops in the War on Terror. With one terrorist bombing attack, Al Qaeda knocked Spain out of the war. It was a despicable act of cowardice by the Spanish people. And it was a terribly dangerous precedent. Now Al Qaeda will focus their efforts on scaring other cowardly European countries out of the war. Soon the United States could stand alone in this war against Islam. But this is simply not right. Europeans might not like it, but this is their fight, too. And they should be fighting with us, not undermining America. It's the same problem the Europeans had with the Nazis. Instead of standing up to bullies, they appeased Hitler and his goons. As a result, we had to fight a massive world war. How massive of a war will America have to fight against Islam because the Europeans refused to stand up to them?

The history of the world shows us that the civilized world is vulnerable to outside attack from the barbarians. Most often, the civilized world is too busy enjoying their lives to see the outside threat for what it is, before it's too late. The Greeks were overrun by the Slavs. The Romans were sacked by the Visigoths. The great Chinese empire was conquered by the Mongols. And if action is not taken against them, Christian Europe

WAKE UP, AMERICA!

could in time be overrun by the radical Muslims, leaving the United States as the lone beacon of freedom and civilization left in the world.

The European policy towards Islam seems to be "if we're nice to them, maybe they'll kill us last." This is a dangerous policy for them, and one that puts the lives of Americans even more at risk.

Missile Defense
★ ★ ★

In 1983, President Reagan called for the United States to develop a ballistic missile defense system to protect America from nuclear weapons. In 1996, the U.S. Congress passed the Defend America Act, which provided that we must develop a National Missile Defense system to counteract the growing threat of nuclear attack.

Despite this Congressional mandate, President Bill Clinton refused to develop a ballistic missile defense system. Clinton follows the classic liberal arguments against the Strategic Defense Initiative (SDI): that it is technologically unfeasible, that it is no longer necessary, and that it violates existing US treaties. But when President George W. Bush took over the White House, he urged a rapid deployment of a national missile defense to protect America from nuclear attack. Though to date no comprehensive national missile defense has been implemented, the need for such protection is greater than ever. With the growing military threat of China, the danger of a nuclear-armed Iran, and the possibility that Islamic terrorists could seize control of a nuclear missile, the United States must develop SDI missile defenses immediately.

This threat is very real and very grave. Remember the destruction leveled against the United States by Al Qaeda terrorists with just a few airplanes: Three thousand Americans dead, the World Trade Center towers in ruins, and the Pentagon severely damaged. Now imagine the death and destruction caused by a nuclear missile launched at an American city. Instead of three thousand dead, there would literally be hundreds of thousands or even millions killed and injured. And instead of a few buildings destroyed, an entire city could be wiped off the face of the map. That is the danger America faces as terrorists and enemy nations work feverishly to get their hands on nuclear weapons. The United States must make it our top priority to implement a missile defense system to protect the country and our people from such a fate.

On March 23, 1983, Ronald Reagan made one of the most important speeches of his presidency. In this speech President Reagan called for the United States to develop a strategic defense system to protect America from nuclear missiles. SDI, the President said, would render nuclear weapons "impotent and obsolete."

This speech was received with considerable surprise and concern. It was thought to represent a radical departure from the long-standing U.S. strategy of deterrence. In fact, however, this initiative was the logical result of the advances in technology (the militarization of space—military satellites, for example—had been underway for years) and the growing public anxiety over nuclear war.

But more than two decades after President Reagan's visionary call to defend America from nuclear missiles, the United States is still completely defenseless against weapons of mass destruction.

It was apparent soon after President Reagan's speech that there would be considerable opposition to SDI from the left. Liberals opposed Ronald Reagan and his policies so vociferously that they were willing to risk leaving the United States completely defenseless from a nuclear attack.

And this continued defenselessness against nuclear missiles is a real and immediate threat to the national security of the United States. The Congress has noted in the *1996 Ballistic Missile Defense Policy Act* that *"the proliferation of ballistic missiles is significant and growing, both quantitatively and qualitatively."* The intelligence community of the United States confirmed that missile proliferation trends are toward longer range and more sophisticated ballistic missiles. Many of these missiles are in the hands of enemies of America, and many of these enemies of America are also developing nuclear weapons.

The post-Cold War international environment is the most dangerous in history regarding the proliferation of weapons of mass destruction (nuclear, biological and chemical) and the ballistic missiles to deliver them. The disintegration of the Soviet Union created four nuclear/ballistic missile states out of one. All four former Soviet Republics (Russia, Ukraine, Byelorussia and Kazakhstan) are cash-strapped and might sell some of this technology to oil-rich—and often radical—Middle Eastern countries or even Islamic terrorists.

In the Third World, countries such as India, Pakistan, Iran and North Korea have either already developed or are developing weapons of mass destruction and the means to deliver them. Regional instability and ethnic strife have increased dramatically since the collapse of communism in 1989-91. This has in turn increased the number of governments seeking weapons of mass destruction and ballistic missiles and the chances that conflict will erupt resulting in the use of these weapons. Since many of these regional conflicts include allies of the United States (Israel and South Korea, for example), it is entirely possible that America would become the target of some missile attack from a hostile Third World nation or Islamic terrorist group.

The proliferation threat has increased dramatically of late. There are five major reasons to be concerned about the increasing threat posed by the spread of nuclear missiles.

First, the number, location and character of the governments of proliferant countries are now highly threatening. The numbers of nuclear-capable countries have doubled in the last 20 years and look to explode in the next 20 years. The likelihood that nuclear missiles are used increases with the number of countries that have them. Further, many of the nations seeking to develop nuclear weapons and ballistic missiles are in unstable regions like the Middle East and the Korean Peninsula, and they are led by aggressive rulers. A nuclear-wielding, militaristic tyrant would be a great threat to American interests.

Second, nuclear missiles in most Third World countries—not to mention Russia or other former Soviet Republics—are not likely to be

either safe or secure. Proper command and control systems over nuclear missiles are both expensive and time consuming. With scant resources already being diverted to research and development of the weapons themselves, there will be little remaining for safeguarding the nuclear missiles. And in those countries that already have nuclear missiles, political instability is cause for concern. In Russia, for example, Chechnyan rebels were able to strike miles into Russian territory undetected. If their target had been a nuclear missile silo, an accidental or unauthorized launch could have occurred during the fighting.

Third, international norms against proliferation are eroding. Treaties and agreements such as the *1925 Geneva Protocol* against chemical weapons, the *Nuclear Non-Proliferation Treaty (NPT) of 1968*, the *Biological/Toxin Weapons Convention of 1972* and the *Missile Technology Control Regime (MTCR) of 1985* have all been violated. There have been several instances of chemical weapons use, the latest being the Iran-Iraq War of 1981-87, where the guilty parties paid little or no penalty for violating a treaty (and Iran is still actively developing nuclear weapons and ballistic missiles). North Korea, Iraq and India have all been documented as violators of the Non-Proliferation Treaty, and many more countries have simply not been caught. Even close American allies like France and Germany have violated the MTCR Treaty by helping Third World dictators develop ballistic missile technology.

Fourth, the development of ballistic missile technology has become as important to many countries as developing nuclear capability. There is a certain amount of prestige that comes with having missile technology, since only the most advanced and sophisticated countries have ballistic missiles. But more importantly, no nation—not even the United States—can defend themselves from these missiles. Aircraft can be shot down, ships sunk and tanks destroyed, but no country can stop a missile. Possession of ballistic missiles gives any country in the world the ability to hurt the United States. Possession of a missile armed with a nuclear warhead gives any country the ability to win a fight with the United States.

Fifth and finally, motivations to acquire nuclear missiles have increased dramatically since the collapse of the Soviet Union and disengagement of the United States. With the guarantee of superpower protection gone with the end of the Cold War, many countries are seeking nuclear weapons themselves. The result is a massive push by many nations to develop or buy this technology as soon as possible.

And there are many who are willing to sell. Experts in missile or nuclear technology from the former U.S.S.R. and Eastern Europe have been reportedly selling their expertise to the highest bidders. And the highest bidders are too often radical regimes hostile to the United States (and possibly even terrorist organizations).

The sale of nuclear and missile technology does not stop there. Cash-strapped nuclear countries often sell their highly coveted technology for the hard currency they desperately need. Russia has repeatedly sold nuclear technology and material to Iran for "peaceful" purposes, and the Russians are actively seeking other buyers. They are also selling "space rocket launchers" to countries who could easily convert them into intercontinental missiles. Communist China has repeatedly sold nuclear technology to Pakistan and has had a large role in North Korea's nuclear development program. And every country knows that China is the place to go for ballistic missiles.

The countries buying nuclear and ballistic missile technology are a disturbing lot. The overwhelming majority of the countries that the U.S. State Department lists as "terrorist" nations are also actively seeking to develop nuclear missiles. Just consider the following two enemies of America:

Iran is a radical Islamic state and major supporter of international terrorism. Iran is very anti-Western and especially anti-American, officially calling America the "Great Satan." It is currently undergoing a massive effort to develop nuclear weapons and ballistic missiles. And the

MISSILE DEFENSE

International Institute for Strategic Studies reported that it was building a nuclear device with Russia and China's help. They are also undergoing efforts to deploy medium range ballistic missiles, with long range missiles soon to come.

The Iranians have done little to keep these programs secret. One Iranian official stated, *"because the enemy [Israel and the United States] has nuclear facilities, the Muslim states should be equipped with the same capacity."* In effect, he was calling on every Arab state to develop nuclear weapons.

Though Iran does not keep its intentions secret, it does keep close guard on its actual program, including the following: undercover activities; spreading of nuclear sites; concealment of installations; creation abroad of networks of agents responsible for the acquisition of nuclear or missile equipment and technology; recruiting of foreign experts from friendly nations such as North Korea, India, China and Pakistan; and persuading Iranian scientists to return from exile (many left when the Ayatollah took power in 1979).

Iran still claims that its nuclear program is for peaceful purposes only, but any examination of that country's role in international terrorism and hostility with its neighbors would strongly suggest otherwise. And remember, Iraq used to claim in the 1980s that their program was also peaceful. Discoveries after the Persian Gulf War proved that, in fact, Saddam's nuclear developments were strictly military.

North Korea is rapidly becoming one of the most significant proliferation threats to the United States in the world. They have been researching nuclear and ballistic missile technology for decades now with the help of Communist China. The primary result of all this effort is a large plutonium-producing nuclear reprocessing plant (which the North Koreans claim to be a radiochemical laboratory). American analysts believe that this plant has been producing nuclear grade plutonium for over a decade. So not only does North Korea have nuclear weapons and the means to deliver them (they have had short and medium range ballistic missiles for years), but they also have an unstable, aggressive political leadership bent on the destruction of South Korea and the American soldiers protecting it.

The United States has had a large military force in South Korea ever since the Korean War armistice. If North Korea has nuclear weapons they can use them against our American troops on the peninsula. This danger has been quite apparent, and the military has long asked for a regional defense system against nuclear missiles. Such a system was developed, but the Clinton Administration blocked deployment, leaving our American soldiers vulnerable to a nuclear attack. Worse, North Korea has been violating the de-militarized zone and renounced the terms of the armistice, clearly provoking a conflict with South Korea and the United States.

It is clear that the proliferation of nuclear weapons and ballistic missiles poses a grave threat to America and our security interests. Though the Cold War is over, the danger of nuclear missile attack is real, and may be greater than ever. The spread of nuclear and ballistic missile technology continues unabated. Internal and regional instability in the former Soviet Union presents the possibility of accidental or unauthorized launch against the United States. Terrorist states in the Third World are actively seeking nuclear missiles themselves. Together, this may pose as great or even greater a threat of nuclear destruction to America than the Soviet Union ever did.

The United States must actively pursue a SDI program to protect itself from these dangers. There are no other viable alternatives. The threat is real and immediate, and we have the means to combat the threat. We must simply make a concerted effort to combat the critics and deploy SDI immediately.

Based on the threat assessment outlined above, the U.S. Congress established the rationale for SDI-type defenses against nuclear weapons, outlined in the Defend America Act of 1996:

MISSILE DEFENSE

- The U.S. has the technical capability to develop and deploy a National Missile Defense system.

- The threat posed to the U.S. by the proliferation of ballistic missiles is growing. The trend is toward longer-range missiles, including those with intercontinental reach.

- There are ways for determined countries to acquire intercontinental ballistic missiles by means other than indigenous development.

- Deployment by the U.S. of a National Missile Defense system will help to deter countries from seeking long-range missiles.

- The danger of an accidental missile launch has not disappeared and deployment of a National Missile Defense system will reduce concerns about this threat.

- Deployment of a National Missile Defense system can enhance stability in the post-Cold War era. The U.S. and Russia should welcome the opportunity to reduce reliance on threats of nuclear retaliation as the sole basis of stability.

- The authors of the Anti-ballistic Missile (ABM) Treaty envisioned the need to change the Treaty as circumstances changed, and they provided the mechanisms to do so in the Treaty. The U.S. and Russia previously considered such changes and should do so again.

The policy of the United States to deploy a nuclear missile defense has already been outlined in the Ballistic Missile Defense Policy Act of 1996. It states that it is the policy of the United States to:

- Deploy as soon as possible highly effective global ballistic missile defenses to counter both the existing and emerging ballistic missiles threat;

WAKE UP, AMERICA!

- Deploy the global missile defense system in such a way that it can be augmented over time to provide a layered defense against larger and more sophisticated ballistic missile threats;

- Pursue a focused research and development program to provide follow-on ballistic missile defense options;

- Employ streamlined acquisition procedures to lower the cost and accelerate the pace of developing and deploying the global defense system;

- Seek a cooperative transition to a regime that does not feature mutual assured destruction and an offense—only form of deterrence as the basis for strategic stability.

Essentially, this act calls for the immediate deployment of an SDI system capable of providing a highly effective defense of U.S. territory against limited, unauthorized or accidental ballistic missile attacks, and which will be augmented to a layered defense as larger and more sophisticated threats emerge.

Based on the evidence of the growing proliferation threat and our defense capabilities, America needs to immediately begin to deploy SDI technologies to protect itself. The facts are clear. There is a growing danger from China, Iran and other Third World nations that a weapon of mass destruction, delivered with a ballistic missile, will be used against America. Without SDI, we could face heavy costs in defending our national interests against states that wield nuclear weapons. The only policy which guarantees defense against nuclear missiles is the deployment of the Strategic Defense Initiative.

CHINA

It is common in America today to think of external enemies exclusively in terms of terrorists and other non-state entities. And while it is true that Al Qaeda and other terrorist organizations are our nation's primary enemies at this time, there is another potential enemy on the horizon that dwarfs the destructive power of Al Qaeda and all the other terrorists put together. That potential enemy is Red China.

Red China is the premier strategic and military threat to U.S. security in the world. It has the largest population in the world, more than four times the population of the U.S.. This massive population allows Red China to put 3 million men on active duty and 12 million more in the reserves, creating the world's largest military force. The army (also the largest in the world) has 2,290,000 men under arms. The navy has 240,000 members, including about 25,000 in the naval air force and another 6,000 in the marines. These naval personnel operate as many as 1700 vessels, including more than 90 submarines, one of them armed with nuclear missiles. The air force has 470,000 members, including 220,000 in air defense. They fly an estimated 5000 combat aircraft (Source: Microsoft Encarta). Red China has 18 inter-continental nuclear missiles, 13 of which are pointed at American cities, and over 100 intermediate and medium range nuclear missiles. And as you can see in Figure 12, Red China's military spending is projected to grow to $350 billion in the next 20 years.

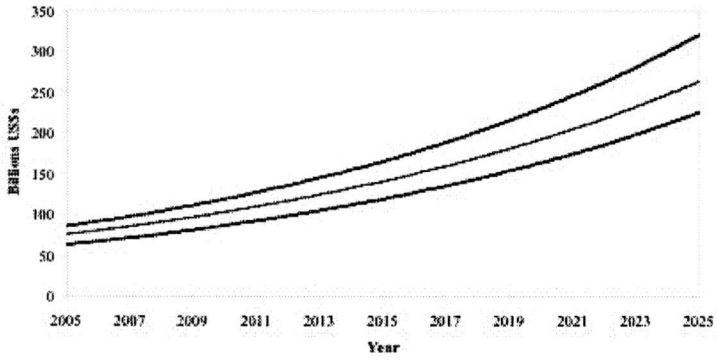

Figure 12. China's Projected Defense Expenditures (Upper, lower and median limits are shown).
Source: www.defenselink.mil

CHINA

China is one of the last remaining communist countries, and as such is still bent on the destruction of capitalism, especially in the United States. And the government in Beijing is still a brutally repressive totalitarian regime which stamps on the rights and liberties of its citizens and foreigners alike. Red China continues to jam the Voice of America, so that their people don't hear information contrary to their propaganda. They refuse to let the International Red Cross have access to their prisons, where most inmates are political prisoners. Political protesters in China are often arrested, and some even disappear, never to be heard from again. Even foreigners are subject to Red China's harsh rule. Anyone caught committing "illegal political activities" like distributing religious pamphlets, for example, are arrested and held for days without being permitted to speak to their embassy. If they're lucky, only their money and possessions are taken from them before they are expelled.

And yet, with all this evidence, the assertion that Red China is the premier military and strategic threat to the U.S. is not universally held. In fact, there is a strong, perhaps even dominant, school of thought in the United States which believes that Red China is one of America's premier strategic and economic partners in the world. Supporters of this school of thought believe it is in America's interest to continue the de facto alliance with China that the U.S. had in the 1970s and 1980s. They tend to be concerned more with economic issues (i.e. doing business in China) and dismiss China's military threats and human rights violations. They support Most Favored Nation status for Red China and believe in "engaging" Beijing to keep them from pursuing a national strategy contrary to American interests.

But the fact of the matter is that China is indeed the prime national security threat to the United States, economics and the de facto alliance notwithstanding. An analogous situation would be the U.S. relationship with the Soviet Union during the Second World War. During the war, the Soviets were our allies against Nazi Germany—the greater threat to both nations at the time. Because both the U.S. and the Soviets were fighting a common enemy, they put their conflicting interests aside for a time. But soon after the defeat of Germany, a U.S.-Soviet rivalry emerged when it became clear the strategic interests of each country were at odds, and the Cold War began.

The American relationship with China in the 1990s is very similar to that American relationship with the Soviet Union. From the early 1970s when President Nixon went to China to the early 1990s, Washington and Beijing had an informal alliance directed against the Soviet Union. Both China and America put their conflicting interests on the back burner to deal with the more serious and imminent threat posed by the Soviets. With the collapse of the Eastern Bloc in 1989-1990 and the disintegration of the Soviet Union in 1992, the strategic partnership between America and China became obsolete. And, as with the U.S. and Soviet Union in 1945, the conflicting strategic interests of each country which were put on the back burner came to the fore.

Strategic Interests in Conflict

So what are these strategic interests, and why are they in conflict? Quite simply, the United States is the dominant power in Asia, and Red China wants to take America's place. America's interests in Asia and the Pacific Rim are many: This region is our fastest growing trading partner in the world;there are vast oil and strategic natural resources available in the region;. and key American allies like Taiwan, Japan and South Korea stand directly in the way of Red Chinese territorial ambitions.

It should come as no surprise that, as Red China builds up its economy, develops its technology, and modernizes its military, it would also seek to expand its sphere of influence in the world and eventually supplant the United States as the dominant power in Asia. Richard Bernstein and Ross H. Munro note in their book, *The Coming Conflict with China*:

Within a few years, China will be the largest economy in the world, and it

CHINA

is on its way to becoming a formidable military power as well, one whose strength and influence are already far greater than those of any other country in the vast Pacific region, except for the United States. China is an unsatisfied and ambitious power whose goal is to dominate Asia...by being so much more powerful than they are that nothing will be allowed to happen in East Asia without China's at least tacit consent.

China's goal, to dominate Asia and the Pacific, is in direct conflict with America's century-long strategic policy of preventing a dominant power from emerging in Asia. From the late 1800s to the early 1900s America's "Open Door" policy regarding China was intended to prevent a European power from dominating East Asia. America's focus shifted to preventing Japan from ascending in Asia in the 1930s, and of course the U.S. fought Japan for supremacy in the Pacific in World War II. During the Cold War, the U.S. aimed to contain Soviet expansion in Asia, and fought wars in Korea and Vietnam to keep the communists out. Today, with the fall of the Soviet Union and the constitutional limits on Japan's military power, only Red China remains to contest with America's power for dominance in Asia. And they are already far down the path of confrontation with America for control of Asia.

China's Three Step Policy

China has always had a specific, three-step policy to begin asserting their power in Asia. The first step was the takeover of Hong Kong, a city on the Chinese mainland which was under British control for 158 years. The second step was the takeover of Macau, a Portuguese possession also on the mainland. Finally, with the historic Chinese mainland under their control, the final step is the takeover of Taiwan, what Red China considers their "rebel" province.

The takeover of Hong Kong, step number one in Red China's emergence as the major Asian power, has already occurred. At midnight, June 30, 1997, the British Colony was formally handed over to Red China, which promised to follow a "one country, two systems" policy allowing freedom and democracy to continue. But China's promise was broken almost immediately. They abolished the duly elected legislature of Hong Kong and put in place a legislature appointed by the Red Chinese. Reports of press censorship emerged. Red China forced several Hong Kong businesses to hand over their companies to Beijing's control for minimum compensation. The Hong Kong police were given new power to control the citizens of Hong Kong, including the right to ban demonstrations. Laws which guaranteed labor rights were suspended. And the election process in Hong Kong was altered to make sure the pro-communist candidates would win. Bernstein and Munro quote an architect of the new system in The Coming Conflict with China:

The design is not simply from the consideration of democratic ideals,' said Lau Siukai, one of the drafters of the new rules who, perhaps unwittingly, admitted the primacy of politics over law.' We have to consider...how to maintain good relations between the mainland and Hong Kong."

The Red Chinese takeover of Hong Kong has been invaluable to the communists. They have gained one of the richest and most impressive economic centers in the world. They have also taken control of a massive deep-water port strategically placed in the South China Sea. And they have gained the international prestige commensurate with the acquisition of such a valuable prize.

Next on Red China's list was Macau, a small Portuguese colony on the Chinese coast. Macau reverted to Red Chinese control in 1999. The takeover of Macau was not the major economic and political event that the takeover of Hong Kong was, to be sure. But the handover of this Portuguese colony still had great significance. With Macau in Red Chinese hands, Beijing now controls all of historical mainland China. And with historical mainland China under their thumb, the communist leadership is free to set their sights on overseas territorial acquisitions—specifically, Taiwan.

CHINA

Taiwan is an island province of China and, since the Communist takeover of the Chinese mainland in 1949, the seat of the government of the Republic of China. It is separated from the Chinese mainland by the Taiwan Strait, but Red China still claims Taiwan as one of its provinces.

On December 8, 1949, following occupation of the mainland by the Communists, the Nationalist government of China, led by General Chiang Kai-shek, established its headquarters on Taiwan. Red China was prevented from invading Taiwan by the United States Navy. In April 1951 the United States further announced that U.S. military personnel would be sent to Taiwan to assist in the training of Nationalist forces. For the remainder of the 1950s, despite sporadic hostilities between Taiwan and the mainland, the United States Navy defended Taiwan from invasion by the Red Chinese. In 1954, the U.S. signed a mutual-defense treaty with Taiwan by which the United States essentially agreed to defend against a Red Chinese attack. Since then, Taiwan has remained an American ally and the source of the greatest friction between Red China and the United States.

This friction came to a head in 1996 when the Red Chinese conducted military "exercises" off the coast of Taiwan, including raining down missiles only miles from the capital of Taiwan. These military exercises were a blatant attempt to influence Taiwan's elections to help get the hard-line anti-communist candidates out of office. In response, the United States sent two U.S. Navy aircraft carriers to the Strait of Taiwan to warn the Red Chinese off. Red China did finally stop their exercises, but not before threatening to destroy Los Angeles with nuclear weapons if America continued its confrontational policies.

This event, the largest military face-off in the Pacific since World War II, could be an ominous sign of things to come. The United States is treaty-bound to defend Taiwan against Red Chinese aggression. America must continue to support Taiwan or else lose international credibility and possibly shatter the entire U.S. alliance structure in the Pacific. But

WAKE UP, AMERICA!

Red China has repeatedly asserted its intent to take over Taiwan—either peacefully or by force—an American security guarantee or not.

Red China wants Taiwan because, of course, they want to re-conquer what they consider to be a rebel province. But Taiwan would also help Red China become the dominant naval power in East Asia in the 21st century. Taiwan sits astride the major strategic sea lanes in East Asia. Most of the commerce going to American allies like Japan and South Korea pass through these sea lanes. The naval and air bases in Taiwan would give Red China the ability to control these strategic sea lanes.

Red China's Military Buildup

Red China's three step policy of taking over Hong Kong, Macau, and Taiwan would put Beijing in a very powerful strategic position. This improved strategic position would help Red China project its growing military power even more, and would facilitate their plan to dominate Asia.

The 2.3-million-man Peoples Liberation Army (PLA) is the dominant branch of the Red Chinese military. They have over 9000 tanks and 14,500 artillery pieces. The PLA is being rapidly reformed to fight effectively in modern battles, stressing flexibility and technological proficiency. Most military regions are building rapid reaction forces of highly mobile and fully equipped units to respond to a crisis or lead an invasion. And the PLA is making a concerted effort to improve their combined arms operations (an attack using the army, navy, and air force all at once to bring maximum firepower to bear)—a prerequisite for an attack on Taiwan or a conflict with the United States.

The impressive stature of the Red Chinese army was in the past mitigated by their weak navy and obsolete air force and a limited ability to project power (i.e., attack) overseas. But the programs to modernize the massive Red Chinese air force and the development of a "blue water" navy have opened the door for China's army throughout the Pacific rim.

Red China's aircraft development program has been the most active in the world in the 1990s. The Red Chinese air force consists of an estimated 5000 planes, many of which are modern attack aircraft based on high quality fighter/bomber Soviet designs.

The most important Red Chinese fighter aircraft is the J-11, a variant of the highly acclaimed Soviet Su-27. These modern attack aircraft have a range of over 1000 miles (depending on refueling) and can drop over 13,000 pounds of bombs on a single run. They can be used to attack targets on land or sea. China will have over 100 of these high quality aircraft in the next few years.

The Red Chinese navy has also undergone a modernization program aimed at producing a "blue water" navy. Blue water navies are capable of operating long distances from base for extended periods of time.

The Red Chinese navy possesses as many as 1700 vessels. Many of these vessels are small, coastal patrol boats. But most of China's naval resources are going toward building larger, modern ships. According to the International Institute for Strategic Studies' "Military Balance," Red China already operates 18 destroyers, 36 frigates, and 90 submarines capable of operating far from China's home ports. And China is working feverishly to expand its blue water navy as rapidly as possible.

Red China's new Luhu-class destroyers have been designed and built specifically to help Beijing take control of the sea in a conflict, presumably with the Taiwanese or American navy. According to Andy Sywak of the Center for Defense Information, these warships have modern guided missile systems for air and surface combat and two French Dauphin helicopters for anti-submarine combat.

Supplementing the Chinese-built Luhu destroyers are the Russian Sovremenny-class destroyers bought in 1997 for $800,000,000. The Center for Defense Information contends that these Russian destroyers *"significantly bolsters [Red China's] long-range offensive capabilities."*

Complimenting the destroyer fleet are the Jiangwei-class frigates. They have guided missile systems and sophisticated radar like the Luhu destroyers, and also have high quality sonar for detecting and attacking enemy submarines.

China's submarines are the strongest arm of Beijing's navy. They have several Kilo-class submarines, one of the best diesel submarines in the world, bought from Russia. They have several more nuclear powered Han-class submarines. And the brand new Song-class submarine is just entering service in the Red Chinese fleet. These formidable nuclear powered submarines will soon be the standard attack boat in Beijing's underwater arsenal.

There should be little doubt as to what this modern blue water naval force will be used for. Former *New York Times* Beijing Bureau Chief Nicholas Kristof predicts that the South China Sea, and specifically Taiwan, will be the most probable place Red China will use its navy. Already, Red China could mount a blockade of Taiwan with its destroyers, frigates, and submarines. And as their navy grows, the possibility increases that Red China could launch an invasion of the island.

The ultimate goal of the Red Chinese navy is to have the ability to contest the United States for control of the seas in the Pacific. Control of the sea will allow the Red Chinese army to threaten territory beyond the Chinese mainland. As Beijing's navy continues to grow and move to build cruisers and aircraft carriers, and as the United States continues to reduce its naval presence in Asia, the possibility of the loss of the Pacific to Red China becomes very real.

For the time being, however, the most dire threat China poses to America comes from their nuclear missiles. The Pentagon's top nuclear war-fighter said that, *"China is engaged in a major nuclear modernization that includes development of multiple-warhead missiles capable of hitting all parts of the United States except southern Florida."*

Right now, Red China has 18 inter-continental nuclear missiles, 13 of which are pointed at American cities. The United States has repeatedly asked Red China to stop targeting their nuclear missiles at the United

States, an agreement that even Russia has made with us. But they have refused to stop targeting their nuclear missiles on us, leaving no doubt about their intentions.

Red China also has an estimated 70 intermediate-range nuclear missiles and 50 medium-range nuclear missiles. These missiles present a growing threat to the United States and its allies, and could potentially be used by China to help even the nuclear balance with America. The use of medium range nuclear missiles in tests off of Taiwan in 1995 and 1996 demonstrates China's willingness to use nuclear intimidation against their adversaries.

Just as bad, Red China is helping other enemies of the United States, and even terrorist countries, develop nuclear missiles of their own that can be targeted at U.S. troops and citizens.

China helped Iran—which calls America the "Great Satan" and held a number of U.S. citizens hostage for 444 days—build long-range Shahab-3 and -4 missiles. They were also caught helping the Iranians with their nuclear development program only weeks after signing an agreement promising not to. China helped North Korea—which started the Korean War that caused over 150,000 casualties—develop their nuclear missile program. And even though they promised not to help Pakistan develop nuclear weapons, China helped Pakistan develop the nuclear weapons they tested in May of 1998 in retaliation to an Indian nuclear test. Thanks to Red China's proliferation of nuclear technology, the Indian Subcontinent is now the scene of the most tense nuclear stand-off since the Cuban Missile Crisis.

Beijing Calls America the Enemy

All the evidence presented so far—the conflict of American and Chinese strategic interests, the tension over Taiwan, building up the military, China's nuclear weapons and proliferation—is convincing enough to most to demonstrate the clear threat Red China poses to the United

WAKE UP, AMERICA!

States. But for those who remain unconvinced, a review of Beijing's own proclamations puts the matter to rest once and for all.

In 1994, a major meeting was held in Beijing's Great Hall of the People. Attending this meeting were high ranking military officials, senior members of the Politburo, propaganda heads of the Communist Party, and representatives from every province of China. Bernstein and Munro report in *The Coming Conflict with China* that the purpose of this major meeting was to, "designate the United States as China's main global rival." General Zhang, Chief of the Army General Staff, said:

"Facing blatant interference by the American hegemonists in our internal affairs and their open support for the debilitating activities of hostile elements inside our country and hostile forces outside the mainland and overseas opposing and subverting our socialist system, we must reinforce the Armed Forces more intensively."

This meeting represented an official and open shift in Red China's policy toward the United States, a shift that is entirely instigated by the Chinese. American policy in Asia has been consistent in the 20th Century: prevent a dominant power from emerging in Asia. The focus of this policy changed over the years, from European colonialists to Japan to the Soviet Union. But the policy remained the same. And this American policy was not in conflict with China's interests for most of the century. Only since the fall of the Soviet Union has this American policy rankled Red China, because they now see an opportunity to dominate Asia themselves. A senior analyst at the Chinese Society for Strategy and Management Research in Beijing said it openly: *"China is growing stronger in the world, and that is affecting the dominant role of the United States ... a fundamental conflict will be inevitable."* (Bernstein and Munro, *The Coming Conflict with China*)

To that end, the Red Chinese military has been preparing for a conflict with the United States. A secret 1993 Red Chinese Army report called *"Can the Chinese Army Win the Next War?"* shows that war with America

CHINA

is the focus of Chinese military planning. The report even goes so far as to conclude that: *China and the United States, focused on their respective economic and political interests in the Asia-Pacific region, will remain in a sustained state of confrontation.*

As Bernstein and Munro state in their book: "*Rarely have Chinese statements been so explicit about the United States being a strategic foe of China, but the idea of the United States as an enemy is far from new.*"

Red China's view of America as an enemy can actually be traced as far back to the Tiananmen Square Massacre in 1989. The Communist leadership in Beijing suspected that the United States inspired and sponsored the pro-democracy student uprising that threatened their power. They pointed to the symbol of the uprising, the Goddess of Democracy, which was a replica of the Statue of Liberty. And when the U.S. suspended high level contacts with Beijing after the crackdown and offered asylum for any student protester who escaped from China, the Communist Party leadership was convinced America was behind the uprising.

A second major historical event which caused a shift in Red China's view of the United States came from the fall of the Soviet Union from 1989-1992. The Soviet Union had been the biggest threat to China's security since the 1960s, and the majority of their military was focused on countering the Russian military. When the Soviet Union collapsed and the military threat from Russia diminished, it freed up the bulk of Red China's military for other duties.

The fall of the Soviet Union also taught the communists in China a very important lesson. Attempts to reform the communist system and ease government oppression, as Gorbachev attempted to do in the Soviet Union, led to disaster. The leadership in Beijing was determined not to let that happen to them. And they viewed the United States as the major source of outside instigation and interference causing unrest in China.

The final major event which caused Red China to change its attitude towards the United States was the Persian Gulf War in 1991. The awesome military power demonstrated by the United States let Red China know just how far behind they were in military doctrine, technology, and operations. Based on the results of the Gulf War, the Chinese knew that they would lose if they came into conflict with the United States. This realization gave new focus to the Chinese military, prompting modernization programs, changes in tactics, and operational adjustments. Evidence of this change can be seen in the development of Red China's missile program. They made a massive effort to improve their long range nuclear missiles so they could credibly threaten the United States. And they embarked on new medium range missile programs, the likes of which were tested off of Taiwan in 1996.

Conclusion

The overwhelming weight of evidence points to the fact that Red China is America's primary enemy in the world. China's goal of domination of Asia is in direct conflict with America's policy of preventing one country from ascending in Asia. And China's specific goal of recapturing Taiwan, America's ally, puts them on a collision course with the United States.

The overwhelming weight of evidence also indicates that Red China's military is doing everything it can to prepare for a war with the United States. They are modernizing their army and adding accurate missiles to their arsenal to increase firepower. They are buying or building every top-of-the-line attack aircraft they can manage. And they are rapidly expanding their blue water navy to project power far from their coastal waters.

Finally, the leadership in Beijing has said for themselves, in their own documents and announcements, that America is their enemy. The 1994 conference in Beijing made it clear that Red China's official policy was to consider the U.S. their "main global rival." And their secret military documents prove that Red China's armed forces are practicing and preparing for a war with the United States of America.

INTERNATIONAL SOCIALISM AND THE UNITED NATIONS
★ ★ ★

Though not a direct military threat, one of the most dangerous external threats to America's economy and culture could very well come from the international socialist movement and their allies at the United Nations. The goal of the international socialists, working through the United Nations, is, for all intents and purposes, to bring the U.S. economy to its knees by forcing America to adopt their failed socialist economic policies. Cliff Kincaid, President of America's Survival, Inc. (www.usasurvival.org), is one of the nation's leading experts on the United Nations and the international socialist movement. What follows is a summary of his reporting on the dangers posed to America from both the United Nations and international socialists.

International Socialism

Both "Socialism" and "Communism" trace their roots to Karl Marx, co-author of *The Communist Manifesto*, who endorsed the first meeting of the Socialist International (SI), then called the "First International."

According to Pierre Mauroy, president of the SI from 1992-1996, *"It was he [Marx] who formally launched it, gave the inaugural address and devised its structure..."* (Pierre Mauroy, A journey to the heart of the Socialist International, 1992-1996, Internationale Socialiste, undated). In 1992, former Soviet President Mikhail Gorbachev addressed the group, and two former Communist parties—including the Italian Democratic Party of the Left—were admitted into membership of the SI.

The Italian Communist Party, which changed its name to Democratic Party of the Left, was admitted into SI membership after the collapse of the Soviet Union, when Communism was exposed to the world as a failed economic system. It had already been exposed as murderous and barbaric. It is interesting to note, however, that its leader, Massimo D'Alema, remained a steadfast Communist even while Communism's bloody and gruesome record grew before him.

Indeed, there is no indication whatsoever that the re-named Italian Communist Party abandoned the basic Communist philosophy. Instead, it simply decided to call it "Socialism." Of course, the old Soviet Communists called themselves "Socialists" too.

Labor connections to the DSA are extensive. A 1996 edition of the DSA's publication, Democratic Left, included words of encouragement, in the form of advertisements, from the following unions:

- The International Union of Electronic, Electrical, Salaried, Machine and Furniture Workers, AFL-CIO.
- Union of Needletrades, Industrial & Textile Employees (UNITE).
- Service Employees International Union (SEIU).
- International Association of Machinists and Aerospace Workers.
- United Steelworkers of America.
- International Union, United Auto Workers.

Democratic Left has referred to Sweeney as "Brother Sweeney," who is, *opening a door to the left, declaring at an end the long Cold War that divided union leadership not only from the now middle-aged radicals of the Sixties generation, but from the gay, feminist, and green activists who define so much that is lively and provocative among the Generation Xers.* (Nelson Lichtenstein, "A Man for Our Season," Democratic Left, September/October 1996, page 5.)

The writer hoped for a resurgence of the power of organized labor, reminiscing about those whose lives were inspired by the Communist takeover in the old Soviet Union: *It's impossible to know if this [Sweeney's] gamble will pay off. In the 1930s, the left was often rooted in America's eth-*

WAKE UP, AMERICA!

nic, working-class communities and full of the self-confidence that grew out of the October Revolution and the seemingly imminent collapse of capitalism. Today, what we used to think of as the traditional, explicitly political left has never been weaker: its revolutionary vision has been dimmed by the Reaganite decades...

At the time of Sweeney's takeover of the AFL-CIO, in collaboration with Richard Trumpka and Linda Chavez-Thompson, the DSA said it would move to "coordinate its local activities more directly with our national allies, including the AFL-CIO and the House Progressive Caucus."

The reference in *Democratic Left* to labor leaders being inspired by the Communist revolution in the old Soviet Union is not just rhetoric. Today, the AFL-CIO associates openly with Communists.

For example, AFL-CIO secretary-treasurer Trumpka spoke to the "Mobilization for Global Justice" rally in Washington on April 16, 2000, and extended greetings, *"and an endorsement of support from the AFL-CIO executive council and its 68 affiliated unions—48 million members of union households in this country."* (As broadcast by C-SPAN, April 16, 2000)

But one wonders if members of these hard-working and over-taxed American families understood that Trumpka was delivering their support for a rally that included the Communist Party USA and many other Communist and Socialist groups as official endorsers. Other endorsers included the DSA, the Foot Fetishists Liberation Front and Queers for Racial and Economic Justice.

Other union leaders speaking at the event included Bobby L. Harnage Sr., national president of the American Federation of Government Employees (AFGE); Edward L. Fire, president of the International Union of Electronic, Electrical, Salaried, Machine and Furniture Workers; George Becker, president of the United Steelworkers of America; and Gerald McEntee, president of the American Federation of State, County and Municipal Employees (AFSCME).

Dump the Debt on Us

The official demands of the protests were "De-fund the Fund," referring to the International Monetary Fund; "Break the Bank," referring to the World Bank; and "Dump the Debt," referring to canceling the debts of Third World countries.

But they have no desire to alter or dismantle the U.N., one of the most corrupt international agencies on the scene.

The ties between the U.N. and the AFL-CIO are quite substantial. Sweeney was a member of the Leadership Council of the Emergency Coalition for U.S. Financial Support of the United Nations, which lobbied for a financial bailout of the U.N. It claimed the backing of all the former secretaries of state, and over 110 business, labor, civic and religious organizations. Other members included James A. Baker III, Henry A. Kissinger, David Rockefeller, George P. Shultz, AFL-CIO chief John Sweeney, Brent Scowcroft, Lawrence S. Eagleburger, former President Jimmy Carter, George J. Mitchell, Alexander M. Haig, Jr., Richard L. Thornburgh and George Soros.

The AFL-CIO is a member of the Council of Organizations that plays a role in the activities of the United Nations Association (UNA-USA), the leading pro-U.N. lobby in the U.S., and Sweeney was the co-editor of a UNA-USA Economic Policy Council book, entitled, *Family and Work: Bridging the Gap.*

The U.N. has played host to meetings of the SI and former U.N. Secretary-General Boutros Boutros-Ghali is a former vice president of the SI.

Leaders of the SI have often been called upon to write reports for the U.N. Mauroy cited a report on disarmament prepared by former Swedish Prime Minister Olof Palme, a report on "sustainable development" by former Norwegian Prime Minister, Gro Harlem Brundtland, and a report on U.N. "reforms" put together by the former Prime Minister of Sweden, Ingvar Carlsson.

WAKE UP, AMERICA!

In 1996, the annual conference of the SI was held in New York at the headquarters of the United Nations. Then—U.N. chief Boutros—Ghali gave the opening speech. AFL-CIO boss Sweeney was also scheduled to speak but didn't show. Sweeney was said to be, *"one of more than 100 labor union leaders expected to attend."* (Betsy Pisik, "The U.N. Report," The Washington Times, August 9, 1996.)

The SI describes itself as "a strong supporter of the UN" (Report of the Secretary General, XX Congress of the Socialist International, United Nations Headquarters, New York 9-11, September 1996, page 74) and has played key roles in various U.N. conferences, including the following:

- The 1992 Earth Summit
- The 1993 World Conference on Human Rights
- The 1995 World Summit for Social Development
- The 1995 Fourth World Conference on Women
- The 1996 U.N. Conference on Human Settlements (Habitat II)

Laying the groundwork for the AFL-CIO's campaign for new management of the global economy, the Paris Declarations of the SI declared:

"We aspire to a new global economic and financial order, which will necessitate some changes in the organizations which were created some 50 years ago, such as the IMF, the World Bank, and the World Trade Organization. None of them have been able to keep up with the changing times, they all require new instruments of prevention and action."

The SI was also "in touch" with the work of the Commission on Global Governance, which considered "the strengthening of international systems of governance."

This commission itself held a series of meetings, beginning in September 1992 and ending in October 1994, which produced a volume entitled Our Global Neighborhood in 1995. The commission included 28 members drawn from 26 countries. The U.S. members were Barber

Conable, former Republican Congressman, and Adele Simmons, President of the MacArthur Foundation. Other members included Oscar Arias, former President of Costa Rica; Hongkoo Lee, Prime Minister of Korea; Brian Urquhart, former U.N. official; and Yuli Vorontsov, Ambassador to the United States and foreign policy adviser to then-Russian President Boris Yeltsin. (Our Global Neighborhood. The Basic Vision, Geneva: The Commission on Global Governance, 1995, page 45.) The summary of the final document stated:

It is time for a consensus on global taxation for servicing the needs of the global neighborhood. A start must be made in establishing schemes of global financing of global purposes, including charges on the use of global resources such as flight-lanes, sea lanes, and ocean fishing areas and the collection of revenues agreed globally and implemented by treaty. An international tax on foreign currency transactions should be explored as one option, as should the creation of an international corporate tax base among multinational corporations. (A Call to Action: Summary of Our Global Neighborhood, the Report of the Commission on Global Governance, Geneva: 1995, page 14.)

In the actual report, the Commission warns that implementing global taxes may be difficult because taxes are generally unpopular and that "even a tightly knit group such as the European Union has not advanced far in tax raising powers." It adds:

The time could be right, however, for a fresh look and a breakthrough in this area. The idea of safeguarding and managing the global commons—particularly those related to the physical environment—is now widely accepted; this cannot happen with a drip-feed approach to financing. And the notion of expanding the role of the United Nations is now accepted in relation to military security. (Our Global Neighborhood, page 217)

The Meltdown of Capitalism

But Sweeney did appear at an April 9, 2000 "Jubilee 2000" demonstration in Washington, D.C., where he committed himself and his giant

WAKE UP, AMERICA!

labor federation to "the goal of debt relief now." (Caryle Murphy, "Joining Hands for Debt Relief," The Washington Post, April 10, 2000, page B1) It sounded like a good cause, but the Jubilee 2000 web site advocated "a completely new economic system" and the "meltdown" of capitalism. Jubilee 2000 said it believes in "the freedom to explore the infinite possibilities inherent in the human condition, something Capitalism will never and can never do." (www.jubilee2000.org/press releases.html#meltdown)

The text of the Jubilee 2000 Project statement, "Preparing for Capitalism's Meltdown," includes the following:

"When the global Ponzi scheme called Capitalism finally collapses because the concentration of wealth has so shriveled consumer spending that it can no longer support the international financial community's expectations of perpetual profits, we better have an alternative ready to take its place if we are to avoid the madness and mayhem that is otherwise certain to follow.

It is that concern that provides one half of the motivation behind The Jubilee 2000 Project. The other half is based upon the conviction that the human race now has the ability to design a completely new economic system that can provide every individual on the planet with, not only the full range of life's necessities, but also the freedom to explore the infinite possibilities inherent in the human condition, something Capitalism will never and can never do.

The objective of the Jubilee 2000 Project is to facilitate the development of just such a design, hopefully before it's too late."

The goal of "debt relief" for the Third World is a cover for global Socialism, under which the financial resources of the United States are transferred abroad. It is more than foreign aid; it is global welfare—a foreign aid giveaway for the purpose of benefiting deadbeat dictators. It is a variation of a global tax.

Thomas Sowell comments, *"The political left's answer to Third World poverty is classic: Let Third World countries welsh on their loans, but don't let them sell the fruits of their labor in the United States, and harass multi-*

national corporations that provide some of the best jobs in poor countries. (Thomas Sowell, "Thoughts on the Passing scene," The New York Post, May 5, 2000, page 35)

He called the approach "crazy."

A different view was offered by Carol Welch, an international policy analyst for Friends of the Earth and a member of the executive committee of Jubilee 2000. *"It was great to get the millions of members of the AFL-CIO on board for debt cancellation,"* she said. Welch estimated the total debt of the third world at $200 billion. (Interview on the Peoples Radio Network, April 14, 2000.) However, G-77 leaders meeting in Havana, Cuba, said it amounts to more than $2.5 trillion. (G-77: Poor Countries Call for Fair Trade, April 17, 2000, UN Wire, quoting Inter Press Service, April 16, 2000)

American taxpayers, Welch acknowledged, will get stuck with much of the bill for debt cancellation because *"The U.S. is the largest shareholder of the World Bank and the IMF,"* the agencies providing the loans to those countries. *"To a certain extent, the U.S. taxpayer will have to pay to cancel those debts,"* she admitted. Some of the *"debt,"* Welch acknowledged, was stolen by foreign leaders and went into their Swiss bank accounts.

The proponents of debt relief have made progress with their campaign because they camouflage it with compassionate and even Biblical language. Many religious groups have joined the campaign as a result. The Jubilee 2000 platform is described as follows:

The Biblical tradition calls for a Jubilee year, when slaves are set free and debts canceled. As the new millennium approaches, we are faced with a particularly significant time for such a Jubilee. Many impoverished countries carry such high levels of debt that economic development is stifled and scarce resources are diverted from health care, education, and other socially beneficial programs to make debt service payments. Much of the debt they carry is the result of ill-conceived development, flawed policies that creditors required of recipient countries in exchange for assistance, and shortsighted decisions of their own leaders. Much of the borrowing benefited only elites in receiving countries, whereas the burden of paying the debt is falling upon the most impoverished members of society.

Recognizing that many of these debts are unpayable and exact a great social and environmental toll, the Jubilee 2000/USA Campaign calls for a time of Jubilee and cancellation of debt that includes:

1. definitive cancellation of the crushing international debt in situations where countries burdened with high levels of human need and environmental distress are unable to meet the basic needs of their people or achieve a level of sustainable development that ensures a decent quality of life;

2. definitive debt cancellation that benefits ordinary people and facilitates their participation in the process of determining the scope, timing and conditions of debt relief, as well as the future direction and priorities of their national and local economies;

3. definitive debt cancellation that is not conditioned on policy reforms that perpetuate or deepen poverty or environmental degradation;

4. acknowledgment of responsibility by both lenders and borrowers, and action to recover resources that were diverted to corrupt regimes, institutions, and individuals;

5. establishment of a transparent and participatory process to develop mechanisms to monitor international monetary flows and prevent recurring destructive cycles of indebtedness.

This platform falls far short of what is required to get these countries in order. The most glaring problem is the failure to hold the "elites" who benefited from the loans and are responsible for corruption.

Welch admitted that the organizers of Jubilee 2000 have no real plan to find or punish those foreign corrupt leaders, except to say that "some form of accountability" through the courts of the various nations might be an option.

It is unclear what the reaction of AFL-CIO members will be when they discover that the head of their labor federation is using their dues money to lobby for a third world bailout, rather than paying down and eliminating the U.S. national debt. The U.S. national debt is now over $5.7 trillion, which figures out to more than $20,000 per American citizen.

Sweeney has not explained that, in the name of "debt relief," his members—and American taxpayers in general—are getting stuck with the bill for a global financial bailout for several dozen corrupt totalitarian socialist states in the Third World, whose leaders have become millionaires and even billionaires.

The concept of "debt relief" constitutes a massive fleecing of U.S. taxpayers.

Declared one keen observer,

Let us not forget that the billions of dollars owed by these countries came from the hard-earned taxes paid by working people in the creditor nations. As a working-class American, imagine your tax dollars being siphoned by some corrupt military or political leader in these countries into their private bank accounts around the world. (Ignatius Anyanwu, "A selective plan for IMF and World Bank debt forgiveness," The Washington Times, April 20, 2000, page A18)

"If debt forgiveness becomes a standing policy for dealing with international debt, what is the incentive to repay sovereign loans?"

The Global New Deal

On February 12, 2000, the campaign for global welfare took a major step forward when U.N. chief Annan proposed a "Global New Deal" for the world. In the U.S., of course, the term "New Deal" has come to represent a dramatic expansion of governmental programs, authority and power, all in the name of helping people.

On the international level, Annan explained that under this new international arrangement, industrialized nations would agree that the, *"benefits"* of globalization would be *"guaranteed"* to other nations *"which stick to an agreed mix of policies designed both to favor investment and to ensure that its benefits are shared by the population as a whole."* He added, *"Can we not attempt on a global level what any successful industrialized country does to help its most disadvantaged or underdeveloped regions catch up?"* (Address by Mr. Kofi Annan, Secretary-General of the United Nations, February 12, 2000. www.unctad-10.org/statements/st_open_annan.en.htm)

What Annan is proposing, without saying so directly, is a global tax scheme to punish Americans and redistribute our money to international bureaucracies and Third World countries.

Going further, Annan said the ultimate goal was:

"enabling all the world's people to participate in the new global economy, and to enjoy its benefits. For that to happen, we need common standards, defined and enforced by States working together in multilateral institutions and, above all, rooted in shared values." (Address by Mr. Kofi Annan, Secretary-General of the United Nations, February 12, 2000. www.unctad-0.org/statements/st_open_annan.en.htm)

These multilateral institutions were identified by Annan as the United Nations Conference on Trade and Development (UNCTAD), the World Bank and the WTO.

Annan may have borrowed the phrase from President Clinton, who spoke of a "Global New Deal" in a speech before the Council on Foreign Relations in 1998 (W. Bowman Cutter, Joan Spero, and Laura D'Andrea Tyson, "New World, New Deal. A Democratic Approach to Globalization," Foreign Affairs, March/April 2000, page 81) or he may have taken it from the AFL-CIO, which called for:

"a global New Deal that establishes new rules to temper the excesses of the market; promote sustainable, egalitarian growth; and assure that the rights of working people everywhere are respected." (U.S. Workers Addressing the Global Crisis, "AFL-CIO Executive Council Statement, October 14, 1998.)

Echoing President Clinton's call for "new financial architecture," the AFL-CIO has said that "cosmetic reform" was not enough, and that "the global economy must be rebuilt from its foundations." It urged "new controls" on the use of financial capital around the world, a "transformed IMF

INTERNATIONAL SOCIALISM AND THE UNITED NATIONS

and World Bank," global debt relief, and "firm, enforceable rules that protect workers' rights, environmental standards, and health and safety..."

In a speech, Sweeney himself called for a "new internationalism," including: *a demand for effective governance that will secure basic worker rights, environmental and consumer protections, sensible anti-trust and financial regulation. (John J. Sweeney, "Making Globalization Work for America," remarks at the Economic Strategy Institute, May 5, 1998)*

He urged "a new internationalist project" and called for trade accords and "international institutions" to "enforce workers' rights [and] environmental protections, not subvert them." He said it was essential that "the United States puts its weight behind" this "new internationalism. There is too much unnecessary short quoting in this section. Should reword things to improve flow.

Like the AFL-CIO, Annan, too, had spoken of new global "financial architecture," telling the so-called "Group of 77" nations and China that the U.N. itself must be "involved in discussions" to bring it about. (John J. Sweeney, "Making Globalization Work for America," remarks at the Economic Strategy Institute, May 5, 1998)

Speaking at a time when an international economic and financial crisis was gripping much of the world, Annan said:

...we have a responsibility, as the universal institution, to stress the global nature of the present crisis—and to insist on the need for global solutions, based on global rules that are fair to all.

All of this is attractive and appealing language designed to usher in a New World Order run by Socialists and Communists and financed largely by global taxes on the American people.

Sweeney's proposed "new controls" over financial capital are the first step toward a global tax.

In this context, New Mexico Senator Jeff Bingaman's proposal for a variation of a global tax to fund liberal initiatives requires explanation and comment. Bingaman, the head of a working group of Senators, prepared this proposal at the request of Senate Democratic Leader Tom Daschle. Bingaman, of course, didn't call it a global tax, and the idea was not put in the form of actual legislation. But his proposal did call for an "A-Fund," financed by a "securities transfer excise tax" (STET), to be enforced on an international basis by the G-7 industrialized countries.

The "A-Fund," which stands for "Financial Markets Allied with America's Businesses and Working Families Fund," is supposed to be one liberal answer to the issue of job insecurity.

Introduced as one part of a 57-page report, *"Scrambling to Pay the Bills: Building Allies for America's Working Families,"* Bingaman proposed a "less-than-one-half-of-one-percent and declining tax" on security sales. By his calculations, it could bring in anywhere from $27 billion to $62 billion a year.

However, it is clear that the tax is not limited to those rich speculators who supposedly have disrupted the financial markets.

The report explains, *"Our proposal would impose a small and diminishing securities transfer excise tax (STET) on broad-based security sales made less than two years after purchase. The tax would extend to transactions by individuals, corporations, and tax-exempt pension funds and other entities and would apply to stocks, bonds, options, futures, and swaps of currency, interest rates, and other assets. This would include trades on behalf of Americans and American assets on American and foreign exchanges, whether done directly or through any intermediary investment fund."*

In other words, ordinary Americans with investments in pension funds, the stock market and IRAs would also pay the financial price.

Some other countries, the report claims, have already imposed "some form" of securities transaction tax. In this case, however, it will have to be global. "To minimize any evasion of the tax in global financial markets, the U.S. should take the lead in the G-7 to coordinate a policy preventing STET evasion," the Bingaman report explains.

This effort to "coordinate a policy" is obviously the beginnings of the effort to implement the tax. The decision to go to the G-7 for support is significant. Studies endorsing global taxes have been underwritten by several G-7 countries, including the governments of Germany, Japan and Canada. France, under its then-Socialist Prime Minister Francois Mitterand, was a big booster of global taxes at the 1995 U.N.-sponsored World Summit for Social Development.

The Senators might point out that they want the revenue from this STET to go for such things as financing tax deductions for higher education, tax credits for children, workforce training, the "school to work" program, and Goals 2000. Some of the revenue, they insist, would also go for "government-industry partnerships" and government export promotion programs.

But what is to prevent such a tax, once it is established, from generating revenues for international bodies like the U.N., the World Bank or the International Monetary Fund? This is a logical next step.

In a 1993 article on "Global Taxation," journalist Martin Walker noted that "the trick" lies in achieving an "international consensus" for it. In regard to a tax on international currency transactions, he said that: *No individual government or trading center dares impose a unilateral tax on its own share of the constant global flow. Any that did would instantly find the business being shifted to more hospitable climes. But an agreement by the dominant G-7 economies, backed up by the OECD [Organization for Economic Cooperation and Development], requiring their own banks and trading houses to comply, should suffice to police such a relatively painless system of exploiting this global resource.* (Martin Walker, "Global Taxation. Paying for Peace," World Policy Journal, World Policy Institute: Vol. X, No. 2, Summer 1993, page 9)

On the implementation of the global *"Tobin tax,"* which Castro endorsed, Mike Prokosch, the director of the global economy program at United for a Fair Economy, has commented that there are *"choke points"* or *"clearing houses"* in such places as New York, Frankfurt and London, "places where the transactions flow through."

WAKE UP, AMERICA!

"It's pretty centralized," he says. "You can enforce your tax through those" financial capitals.

Section VI: Solutions

Throughout this book, suggestions have often been made to correct specific problems discussed in each chapter. And they are all good solutions to those specific problems. However, these are all symptoms of the greater disease. And to truly heal our nation of this vile degeneration, Americans must directly confront the secular-socialist forces that seek to undermine your liberty, tear down our capitalist system, and eat away at our traditional Christian heritage. In other words, Americans must fight back against those who are trying to turn us into Europeans.

We have two enemies in this war: the liberal secular-socialist elites (both within and without the country) and the ignorance and apathy of the American people. The secular-socialists are leading the charge to take away our liberty, undermine our economic system and stamp religion out of public life. The ignorant and apathetic are the people in America who refuse to believe or refuse to care that the pillars of greatness in America are under assault. We must fight back against the first group in this war. And we must educate the second group to the dangers, bring them onto God's side, and together rescue our great nation.

In the battle against ignorance and apathy, we need to educate (or re-educate) more citizens, elected officials and appointed judges about the liberties guaranteed in the Constitution, the fundamental benefits of our capitalist economic system, and the true meaning of separation of church and state. Until we win the philosophical battle and shine the light of truth on these issues, secular-socialist forces will continue to win these battles. Only by educating and rallying as many Americans as possible to our cause can we win this fight.

In the matter of direct action against secular-socialists, Americans must begin to actively support those policies that reinforce our liberty, economy and religious heritage. For example, Americans need to fight at the local, state and federal level to reverse the disastrous Supreme Court ruling allowing government to seize your private property—not for public use, but to hand it over to others who will pay the government more taxes. This is a fundamental battle for your individual liberty. Americans also need to press elected officials at the local, state and federal level to scale back the massive government intrusion into our lives, and the huge taxes we have to pay to sustain this leviathan government. The less government intrusion into our lives, the stronger our individual liberty will be. And the less government intrusion and taxes the American people face, the stronger our capitalist economic system will be. Americans of faith need to make it a focus both of their political activism and their voting habits that only small-government, lower-taxing fiscal conservatives who understand the Constitution as it was originally written get elected into public office.

In the matter of our Christian heritage, Americans of faith need to systematically restore the rights secular-socialists have stolen from us over the past forty-plus years. For just one example, an amendment to the Constitution to permit voluntary school prayer is desperately needed to help overcome opposition to religion in public life. Writing in the Charlotte Observer, Dr. Norman Geisler, Dean of the Southern Evangelical Seminary in Charlotte, NC outlined ten critical reasons why such an amendment is necessary::

1. Our government was based on religious principles from the very beginning. The Declaration of Independence says: *"We hold these truths to be self-evident, that all men are created equal, that they are endowed by God with certain unalienable rights..."*. Indeed, it speaks of God, creations, God-given moral rights, the providence of God, and a final Day of Judgment—all of which are religious teachings. Indeed, the Supreme Court affirmed (Zorach, 1952) that, *"We are a religious people whose insti-*

tutions presuppose a Supreme Being.". And school prayer has been an important part of our religious experience from the very beginning.

2. The First Amendment does not separate God and government but actually encourages religion. It reads: *"Congress shall make no law respecting the establishment of religion, nor prohibiting the free exercise thereof."* The first clause merely declares that the federal government cannot establish one religion for all the people. It says nothing about "separation of church and state." In fact, five of the 13 states that ratified it had their own state religions at the time. The second clause insists that the government should do nothing to discourage religion. But forbidding prayer in schools discourages religion.

3. Early congressional actions encouraged religion in public schools. For example, the Northwest Treaty (1787 and 1789) declared: *"Religion, morality, and knowledge being necessary for good government and the happiness of mankind, schools and the means of learning shall forever be encouraged."* Thus, religion, which includes prayer, was deemed to be necessary.

4. Early presidents, with congressional approval, made proclamations encouraging public prayer. President Washington on October 3, 1789, declared: *"Whereas it is the duty of all nations to acknowledge the providence of Almighty God, to obey His will, to be grateful for His benefits, and humbly to implore His protection and favor; and Whereas both Houses of Congress have, by their joint committee, requested me 'to recommend to the people of the United States a day of public thanksgiving and prayer..."*

5. Congress has prayed at the opening of every session since the very beginning. Indeed, in a moment of crisis at the very first Continental Congress, Benjamin Franklin urged prayer and observed, *"In the beginning of the Contest with G. Britain, when we were sensible to danger, we had daily prayer in this room for Divine protection—Our prayers, Sir, were*

heard, & they were graciously answered... And have we now forgotten that powerful Friend? or do we imagine we no longer need His assistance? ...I therefore beg leave to move—that henceforth prayer imploring the assistance of Heaven, and its blessing on our deliberations, be held in this Assembly every morning before we proceed to business, and that one or more of the clergy of this city be requested to officiate in that service." Congress has begun with prayer ever since. If the government can pray in their session, why can't the governed pray in their (school) sessions?

6. Public schools had prayer for nearly 200 years before the Supreme Court ruled that state-mandated class prayers were unconstitutional (Engle, 1962). The fact that prayer was practiced for nearly 200 years establishes it by precedent as a valid and beneficial practice in our schools.

7. Since the court outlawed prayer, the nation has been in steady moral decline. Former Secretary of Education William Bennet revealed in his cultural indexes that between 1960 and 1990 there was a steady moral decline. During this period divorce doubled, teenage pregnancy went up 200%, teen suicide increased 300%, child abuse reached an all-time high, violent crime went up 500% and abortion increased 1000%. There is a strong correlation between the expulsion of prayer from our schools and the decline in morality.

8. Morals must be taught, and they cannot properly be taught without religion. There cannot be a moral law without a moral Law Giver. And there is no motivation for keeping the moral law unless there is a moral Law Giver who can enforce it by rewards and punishments.

9. Forbidding prayer and other religious expressions in public schools establishes, in effect, the religion of secularism. The Supreme Court has affirmed that there are religions, such as "secular humanism," which do not believe in God. Justice Potter rightly feared that purging the schools

of all religious beliefs and practices would lead to the "establishment of a religion of secularism." In fact, the beliefs of secular humanism are just the opposite of the Declaration of Independence. By not allowing theistic religious expression, the courts have favored the religious beliefs of secular humanism, namely, no belief in God, God-given moral laws, prayer and a Day of Judgment.

10. To forbid the majority the right to prayer because the minority object, is to impose the irreligion of the minority on the religious majority. Forbidding prayer in schools, which a three-quarters majority of Americans favors, is the tyranny of the minority. It is minority rule, not democracy. Why should an irreligious minority dictate what the majority can do? The majority wishes to preserve our moral and spiritual values and, thus, our good nation.

Though it will take a great deal of work, such a constitutional amendment is urgently needed to restore our children's fundamental right to pray in public schools. Nothing short of an amendment will do, in order to circumvent the liberal judges that so often side with the secular-socialist forces to impose their perverse will on the rest of us. But the good news is this—if an overwhelming groundswell of Christians rise up and demand this, it will be amazing how fast the politicians crawl over each other in order to help get this amendment passed.

Speaking of those liberal judges working with the secular-socialists to thwart the will of average Americans, we must overcome this insipid force in America as well. Traditional Values Coalition, a non-profit Christian organization located in Washington, D.C., has proposed an excellent five-point plan to combat judicial tyranny:

FIRST: We must limit the appellate jurisdiction of the U.S. Supreme Court. The U.S. Constitution, Article III, Section 2, states that "the

Supreme Court shall have appellate jurisdiction, both as to law and fact, with such exceptions, and under such regulations as the Congress shall make." Under this provision of the Constitution, Congress can prohibit the Court from cases involving such issues as abortion, homosexuality, school prayer, pornography, the Ten Commandments, etc.

SECOND: Under Article III, Section 1 of the Constitution, Congress has the power to create or abolish federal courts. Congress can also cut off salaries to renegade judges and their staffs. Congress also has the power to abolish federal judgeships outright, and they should do just that to make it clear that judicial usurpation will not be allowed. A judge who knew his position would be abolished might be more restrained in his rulings.

THIRD: The Constitution provides in Article III, Section 2 that judges can remain in power as long as they are on "good behavior." The Constitution provides for the impeachment of judges who fail to fulfill their duties. Grounds for impeachment are broad in the Constitution. We should urge impeachment proceedings against out-of-control judges.

FOURTH: State judges, who are appointed, should be elected by the people in their states. They should not have lifetime positions. They should be forced to face the electorate so they will remain accountable.

FIFTH: We must elect local, state, and federal officials who respect the Constitution and who will curtail the power of renegade judges! Currently, we do not live under a rule of law but the rule of tyrants. Most urgently, we must make sure the Senate confirms as many conservative judges as possible this year to replace those liberal judicial activists on the bench right now.

Traditional Values Coalition's five point plan is an excellent one. They should be commended for their leadership in this arena as well as supported for their work. And there are many other concrete actions that Americans of faith can take to help restore the pillars of greatness in the United States. Laws have been proposed in many states banning any government entities from seizing private property. These laws should be passed! The 2001 major tax cuts passed by Congress are set to expire in 2011. Congress should make these tax cuts permanent, and cut the taxes of the American people even more. Right now there is an amendment working its way through Congress (called H.J. Res. 57) that would protect religious freedom and restore the rights of Christians taken away by the secular-socialists. Americans should press their elected officials to pass this Religious Freedom Amendment! Marriage Protection Amendments have been discussed in all 50 states, to protect traditional families and the institution of marriage from the assault of secular-socialists. State officials should support these amendments as well. In sum, Americans of faith need to get active themselves, and in turn make their views known to those who are supposed to represent us in government. When Americans of faith fail to stand up and take action, the only voices our politicians will hear will be those of the secular socialists. That's why America is in so much trouble in the first place.

Simply stated, God will not bless a secular-socialist nation. We have already seen that in the terrorist attacks on our nation. And we all need to realize that the future will be even more grim unless we restore individual liberty, buttress our capitalist system, and return to our Christian heritage. When a nation loses more people in one morning from terrorist attacks than in any day during the Second World War, something is terribly wrong in America. As you have just read, there are many concrete actions you can take to help restore the institutions that made America great and by extension return our nation to God's grace.

Section VI: Solutions

Returning to God

In the other chapter of this section on solutions, we discuss many concrete examples of what Americans can do to help save the United States from ruin. But fundamentally, to really rescue our nation and return it to our former status as a city on a hill, Americans must once again turn our lives over to God. One of the single most alarming trends in the United States is the increasing number of people who have never been to church (Figure 13). Without a strong moral foundation upon which to fall back, it's much easier for the secular-socialist forces in America to convince, connive and browbeat average Americans into accepting their dangerous philosophies. One of the most important aspects of religion is the strong, black-and-white sense of right and wrong. Americans who go to church have this strong sense of right and wrong. Those who've never been to church do not, and can easily be led astray by the forces of secular socialism. This is exactly why the secular-socialists try so hard to stamp all aspects of religion out of public life. The less religion there is in America, the less opposition to their cause. So one of the fundamental solutions to the problems our nation faces today is simply to get more Americans to attend church and learn about God and faith.

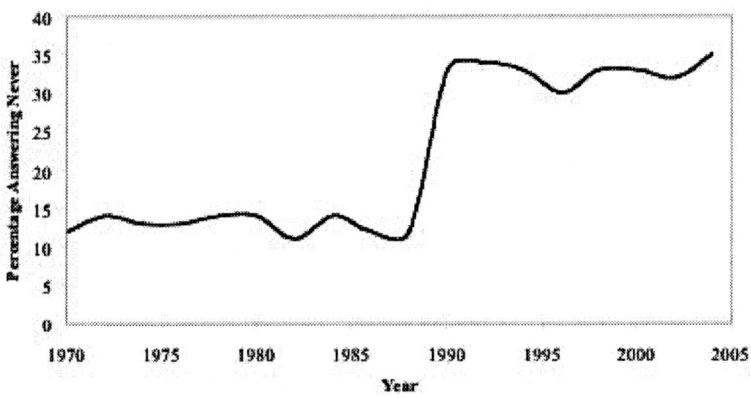

Figure 13. Americans Who Do Not Attend Church.
Source: The American National Election Studies

RETURNING TO GOD

How to Make Christ Your Personal Lord and Savior

Jesus Christ, the Son of the living God, came to earth to die for our sins and to offer you a plan for salvation. When Jesus died upon the cross, He accepted all of your sins and He took your punishment by laying down His own life.

Why did He do such a thing? It was part of God's plan of salvation for Jesus to take your place upon the cross to offer you the opportunity for eternal life. You cannot earn salvation by your good deeds here on this earth. You can only be granted salvation by accepting Jesus, repenting of your sins and then living a life that honors God. If you want to be a Christian you have to study His word and understand what it means to be a true Christian.

Salvation is a free gift from our heavenly Father, but we do have to ask for that gift in order to receive it. Salvation is as sure as the sun rising in the east tomorrow, but you have to find out what God expects from you and then be obedient to his word. Once you commit to becoming a Christian you will learn more about living a Christian life and having a personal relationship with Jesus Christ. He is an ever-present force in your life and He is available to help you in a time of trouble.

The Bible tells us in Acts 2:21, "Whosoever shall call upon the name of the Lord shall be saved." In Romans 10:9 the Bible explains, "If thou shalt confess with thy mouth the Lord Jesus and shalt believe in thine heart that God raised Him from the dead thou shalt be saved."

First pray this prayer and receive Jesus as your personal Lord and Savior. When you pray this prayer you are accepting Jesus into your life and He becomes your Lord.

Dear Lord, I am calling upon you. I am praying and asking Jesus Christ to come into my heart and be Lord over my life. I confess with my mouth that Jesus is my Lord and Savior. I believe in my heart that He died upon the cross and God raised Him from the dead to offer me a plan for salvation. I pray that you will reveal more of the Christian walk to me every day. Amen.

WAKE UP, AMERICA!

Now that you have taken the first step and have recognized Jesus Christ as your Savior you need to repent of your past sins and turn away from your old ways. Find a Bible-believing Church and become part of the family of God. Get a Bible and read it every day so that you gain an understanding of what God expects. Be obedient to His word and you will "work out" your salvation.

Only when you are personally saved can you then truly work to save our nation. In fact, our nation gets closer to rescue each and every time another American simply accepts Jesus as his Lord and Savior. As the army of Christians grows in America, the size of the opposition to secular-socialists will grow commensurately. And together, we can defeat this pernicious force in our country and restore America as the godly nation we once were. I hope and pray you will stand with me in this most important endeavor.

God bless you and Amen.

Returning to God

What You Can Do

This book was not published by one of the big publishing houses in New York. It was published and distributed by the nonprofit Caudill Foundation as part of our education and outreach program. But this book is not the limit of our program. As we discussed in the section on solutions, we need to educate people about the dangers America faces in order to rally them to our cause. This education project is one of the main programs of the Caudill Foundation. But such a massive project does not come cheaply. We need funds to continue to print and distribute copies of this book, educational pamphlets, and many other pieces of literature. We also need funds to promote the work of this foundation and our ministry, both of which seek to restore America to her position of greatness by returning to the foundation and principles of God in Christ.

You can contact us directly for more information about *The Caudill Charitable Foundation*. You can also order more copies of this book at:

www.caudillfoundation.com

or write us at:

The Caudill Charitable Foundation
1000a Kendras Run
Gallatin, TN 37066

The Caudill Charitable Foundation is a 501c3 charitable foundation. Your donations are tax deductible. I urge you to consider a donation to help Restore America's Godly Heritage.

About the Author

Kip's life is an unusual story. Born into a highly respected family, the only child of Noble and Venorice Caudill, Kip grew up in the money centers of America—New York, Boston, Washington, Chicago and Miami—traveling with his father who was both treasurer and finance chairman of a billion dollar world conglomerate as well as the finance chairman for Senator Estes Kefauver in his bid for the U.S. presidency in 1952 and 1956. Kip's background is extremely varied. He holds records in baseball, downhill skiing and auto racing. He is a pilot of high performance aircraft, he has raced thoroughbreds, and has owned oil and gas production and a drilling equipment company. In addition, he was a major stockholder in family banking, owner of a commercial real estate brokerage company, a seasoned land developer and investor, builder of commercial income properties, securities investor, multiple farm owner, and political fund raiser and adviser. Kip has served on various boards, and after living a life for many years as an adventurer and bachelor, made a commitment to Christ and the Christian worldview to build a Christian foundation for the purpose of honoring Christ and His teachings, and to restore America's godly heritage. He has spent years as a spirit-filled Christian studying the Bible, America's founding documents, the lives of the founders, the Christian worldview and the history of America.

Appendix
Invocations of God in Presidential Inaugurations

George Washington, 1789
"... *the benign Parent of the Human Race ... has been pleased to favor the American people with opportunities [for] the security of their union and the advancement of their happiness... The success of this Government must depend[upon]? His divine blessing.*"

John Adams, 1797
Invoking the Supreme Being, "*Patron of Order, Fountain of Justice, and Protector in all ages...of virtuous liberty*" to continue "*His blessing upon this nation...and give it all possible success and duration consistent with the ends of His providence.*"

Thomas Jefferson, 1801
"*May that Infinite Power which rules the destinies of the universe lead our councils to do what is best...for peace and prosperity.*"

Jefferson, 1805
"*that Being in whose hands we are...who has covered our infancy with His providence and our riper years with His wisdom and power...so that He will so enlighten...your servants, guide their councils, so they shall do your good and secure the peace, friendship, and approbation of all nations.*"

James Madison, 1809
Beseeched, "*the guidance of that Almighty Being whose power regulates the destiny of nations, whose blessings*" have enriched "*this rising Republic.*"

James Monroe, 1817
Invoked, "*the Almighty that He will...continue...that protection...He has already so conspicuously displayed.*"

WAKE UP, AMERICA!

Monroe, 1821
"... firm reliance on the protection of Almighty God ..."

John Quincy Adams, 1825
Invoked the Lord's favor and, *"His overruling providence"*.

Andrew Jackson, 1829
Expressed reliance on, *"that Power whose providence mercifully protected our nation's infancy, and has since upheld our liberties"* and beseeched Him to *"continue to make our beloved country the object of His divine care."*

Andrew Jackson, 1833
Beseeched *"that Almighty Being"* to *"overrule all my intentions and actions and inspire the hearts of my fellow citizens that we may be preserved from dangers...and continue forever as a united and happy people."*

Martin Van Buren, 1837
Beseeched *"His providence to bless our beloved country with honors and with lengths of days."*

William Henry Harrison, 1841
Expressed *"profound reverence to the Christian religion,"* convinced that *"sound morals, religious liberty, and just a sense of religious respectability are essentially connected with all true and lasting happiness"* and commended us to *"that good Being who has blessed us by the gifts of civil and religious liberty."*

James K. Polk, 1845
Invoked *"that Divine Being"* who has protected us, and beseeched his continued *"benedictions."*

WAKE UP, AMERICA!

Zachary Taylor, 1849
Invoked, *"the goodness (and protection) of Divine Providence."*

Franklin Pierce, 1853
Invoked, *"the kind Providence"* which enabled us to preserve our blessings.

James Buchanan, 1857
Invoked, *"the blessings of Divine Providence."*

Abraham Lincoln, 1861
Speaking of opponents dissatisfied with the government, Lincoln called for, *"Intelligence, patriotism, Christianity, and a firm reliance on Him who has never yet forsaken this favored land…"*

Abraham Lincoln, 1865
Both sides in the conflict "read the same Bible and pray to the same God, and each invokes His aid against the other. It may seem strange that any men should dare to ask a just God's assistance in wringing their bread from the sweat of other men's faces, but let us judge not, that we be not judged. The prayers of both could not be answered. That of neither has been answered fully. The Almighty has His own purposes. 'Woe unto the world because of offenses [and] woe to that man by whom the offense cometh.' If we shall suppose that American slavery is one of those offenses which, in the providence of God, must needs come, but which, having continued through His appointed time, He now wills to remove, and that He gives to both North and South this terrible war as the woe due to those [who commit the offense], shall we discern therein any departure from those divine attributes which believers in a living God always ascribe to Him? Fondly do we hope, fervently do we pray, that this mighty scourge of war may speedily pass away."
"With malice toward none, with charity for all, with firmness in the right as God gives us to see the right, let us strive to finish the work we are in, to bind

up the nation's wounds, to care for him who shall have borne the battle and for his widow and his orphan, to do all which may achieve and cherish a just and lasting peace among ourselves and with all nations."

Ulysses S. Grant, 1869
Invokes, *"almighty God"* to heal the nation.

Rutherford B. Hayes, 1877
Invokes *"guidance of that Divine Hand by which the destinies of all nations and individuals are shaped"* so that *"peace and happiness, truth and justice, religion and piety, may be established among us for all generations."*

James A. Garfield, 1881
"I reverently invoke the support and blessings of Almighty God for the welfare of this great people."

Grover Cleveland, 1885
Invokes aid and blessings of, *"Almighty God, who presides over the destiny of nations..."*

Benjamin Harrison, 1889
"God has placed upon our head a diadem and laid at our feet power and wealth beyond definition or calculation, a beacon of hope for the freedom of all peoples."

Grover Cleveland, 1893
"A Supreme Being who rules the affairs of men and nations...will not turn from us now if we humbly and reverently seek His powerful aid."

William McKinley, 1897
Swore *"before the Lord Most High"* to seek by *"constant prayer"* to dis-

WAKE UP, AMERICA!

charge *"my solemn responsibilities"*.

William H. Taft, 1909
Sought the, *"aid of Almighty God in the discharge of my responsible duties."*

Woodrow Wilson, 1913
"I summon all honest men, all patriotic, all forward-looking men, to my side. God helping me, I will not fail them ..."

Woodrow Wilson, 1917
He invoked, *"God's Providence"* to purge fractional divisions of party and private interests and *"I pray God I may be given the wisdom and prudence to do my duty."*

Warren G. Harding, 1921
Spoke of *"the God-given destiny of our Republic,"* was *"answerable to God and country,"* and implored the *"favor and guidance of God in His Heaven."* I have taken the oath on *"that passage of Holy Writ: 'What doth the Lord require of thee but to do justly, and to love mercy, and to walk humbly with thy God?' This I plight to God and country."*

Calvin Coolidge, 1925
"America seeks no earthly empire built on blood and force... The legions which we send forth are armed, not with the sword, but with the cross...all mankind [is] of divine origin. She cherishes no purpose save to merit the favor of Almighty God."

Herbert Hoover, 1929
"I ask the help of Almighty God."

WAKE UP, AMERICA!

Franklin D. Roosevelt, 1933
Asked, *"the blessing of God...May He guide me in the days to come."*

Franklin D. Roosevelt, 1937
Asked, *"Divine guidance to help us each and every one..."*

Franklin D. Roosevelt, 1941
"As Americans, we go forward, in the service of our country, by the will of God."

Franklin D. Roosevelt, 1945
"The Almighty God has blessed our land [and has given us] a faith which has become the hope of all peoples in an anguished world. So we pray to Him [for] the achievement of His will."

Harry S. Truman, 1949
"Steadfast in our faith in the Almighty, we will advance toward a world where man's freedom is secure... With God's help, the future of mankind will be assured in a world of justice, harmony, and peace."

Dwight D. Eisenhower, 1953
In this, *"century of trial"* we pray to, *"Almighty God."*

John F. Kennedy, 1961
Asking, *"His blessing and His help ... knowing that here on earth God's work must truly be our own."*

Lyndon B. Johnson, 1965
"But we have no promise from God that our greatness will endure...democracy rests on faith [and] the judgment of God is harshest on those who are most favored."

WAKE UP, AMERICA!

Richard M. Nixon, 1969

"As the Apollo astronauts flew over the moon's gray surface on Christmas Eve…we heard them invoke God's blessing on [the earth's] goodness…let us go forward, firm in our faith [and] sustained by our confidence in the will of God and the promise of man."

Richard M. Nixon, 1973

"Sustained by our faith in God who created us, and striving always to serve His purposes."

Jimmy Carter, 1977

No reference, but took oath of office on Bible opened to passage, *"What doth the Lord require of thee, but to do justly, and to love mercy, and to walk humbly with thy God."* Micah 6:8

Ronald Reagan, 1981

"With God's help, we can and will resolve our problems. God bless you."

Ronald Reagan, 1985

"We stand today One people under God…We have moved toward the 'brotherhood of man' that God intended for us…may He continue to hold us close…one people under God, dedicated [to freedom]…God bless you and may God bless America."

George H.W. Bush, 1989

"My first act as President is a prayer. I ask you to bow your heads: Heavenly Father, accept our thanks for the peace that yields this day…Make us strong to do Your work, willing to heed and hear Your will…We are given power not to advance our own purposes…There is but one just use of power, and it is to serve people. Help us to remember it, Lord. Amen. God bless you and God bless the United States of America."

WAKE UP, AMERICA!

Bill Clinton, 1993

"The Scripture says, 'And let us not be weary in well-doing.'... With God's help, we must answer the call... God bless you all."

Bill Clinton, 1997

"May God strengthen our hands for the good work ahead, and always, always bless our America."

George W. Bush, 2001

"I know this is in our reach because we are guided by a power larger than ourselves who creates us equal in His image."

George W. Bush, 2005

"From the day of our founding, we have proclaimed that every man and woman on this Earth has rights, and dignity and matchless value because they bear the image of the maker of heaven and Earth."

SOURCE: U.S. Government Printing Offices' Inaugural Addresses of Presidents of the United States (Washington to Nixon) and White House Archives.

Printed in the United States
65238LVS00002B/139-300